THE
SLOVAK
AMERICANS

THE
SLOVAK
AMERICANS

M. Mark Stolarik

CHELSEA HOUSE PUBLISHERS

New York   New Haven   Philadelphia

Cover Photo: Slovak immigrants arrive in the New World at the turn of the century.

Editor-in-Chief: Nancy Toff
Executive Editor: Remmel T. Nunn
Managing Editor: Karyn Gullen Browne
Copy Chief: Juliann Barbato
Picture Editor: Adrian G. Allen
Art Director: Giannella Garrett
Manufacturing Manager: Gerald Levine

Staff for Slovak Americans

Senior Editor: Sam Tanenhaus
Text Editor: Constance Jones
Assistant Editor: Abigail Meisel
Editorial Assistant: Theodore Keyes
Copyeditor: James Guiry
Designer: Noreen M. Lamb
Layout: Louise Lippin
Production Coordinator: Joseph Romano
Cover Illustration: Paul Biniasz
Banner Design: Hrana L. Janto

Creative Director: Harold Steinberg

Library of Congress Cataloging-in-Publication Data

Stolarik, M. Mark, 1943–
  The Slovak Americans

  (The Peoples of North America)
  Bibliography: p.
  Includes index.
  Summary: Discusses the history, culture, and religion of the Slovaks, factors encouraging
their emigration, and their acceptance as an ethnic group in North America.
    1. Slovak Americans—Juvenile literature. [1. Slovak
Americans] I. Title. II. Series.
E184.S64S75   1988   973'.049187   87-15872

ISBN 1-55546-134-4   325.2

CONTENTS

Introduction: "A Nation of Nations" 7

From Farm to Factory 13

A Brief History of Slovakia 17

Arriving in the New World 33

The Community Grows 45

Picture Essay 49

Ordinary Days and Holidays 67

Cultural Vitality 83

The Slovak Community Today 95

Further Reading 106

Index 107

THE PEOPLES OF NORTH AMERICA

THE IMMIGRANT EXPERIENCE
ILLEGAL ALIENS
IMMIGRANTS WHO RETURNED HOME
THE AFRO-AMERICANS
THE AMERICAN INDIANS
THE AMISH
THE ARAB AMERICANS
THE ARMENIAN AMERICANS
THE BALTIC AMERICANS
THE BULGARIAN AMERICANS
THE CARPATHO-RUSYN AMERICANS
THE CENTRAL AMERICANS
THE CHINESE AMERICANS
THE CROATIAN AMERICANS
THE CUBAN AMERICANS
THE CZECH AMERICANS
THE DANISH AMERICANS
THE DOMINICAN AMERICANS
THE DUTCH AMERICANS
THE ENGLISH AMERICANS
THE FILIPINO AMERICANS
THE FRENCH AMERICANS
THE FRENCH CANADIANS
THE GERMAN AMERICANS
THE GREEK AMERICANS
THE HAITIAN AMERICANS

THE HUNGARIAN AMERICANS
THE IBERIAN AMERICANS
THE INDO-AMERICANS
THE INDO-CHINESE AMERICANS
THE IRANIAN AMERICANS
THE IRISH AMERICANS
THE ITALIAN AMERICANS
THE JAPANESE AMERICANS
THE JEWISH AMERICANS
THE KOREAN AMERICANS
THE MEXICAN AMERICANS
THE NORWEGIAN AMERICANS
THE PACIFIC ISLANDERS
THE PEOPLES OF THE ARCTIC
THE POLISH AMERICANS
THE PUERTO RICANS
THE ROMANIAN AMERICANS
THE RUSSIAN AMERICANS
THE SCOTCH-IRISH AMERICANS
THE SCOTTISH AMERICANS
THE SERBIAN AMERICANS
THE SLOVAK AMERICANS
THE SOUTH AMERICANS
THE SWEDISH AMERICANS
THE TURKISH AMERICANS
THE UKRAINIAN AMERICANS
THE WEST INDIAN AMERICANS

CHELSEA HOUSE PUBLISHERS

A
NATION
OF
NATIONS

Daniel Patrick Moynihan

The Constitution of the United States begins: "We the People of the United States . . ." Yet, as we know, the United States is not made up of a single group of people. It is made up of many peoples. Immigrants from Europe, Asia, Africa, and Central and South America settled in North America seeking a new life filled with opportunities unavailable in their homeland. Coming from many nations, they forged one nation and made it their own. More than 100 years ago, Walt Whitman expressed this perception of America as a melting pot: "Here is not merely a nation, but a teeming Nation of nations."

Although the ingenuity and acts of courage of these immigrants, our ancestors, shaped the North American way of life, we sometimes take their contributions for granted. This fine series, *The Peoples of North America*, examines the experiences and contributions of the immigrants and how these contributions determined the future of the United States and Canada.

Immigrants did not abandon their ethnic traditions when they reached the shores of North America. Each ethnic group had its own customs and traditions, and each brought different experiences, accomplishments, skills, values, styles of dress, and tastes in food that lingered long after its arrival. Yet this profusion of differences created a singularity, or bond, among the immigrants.

The United States and Canada are unusual in this respect. Whereas religious and ethnic differences have sparked intolerance throughout the rest of the world—from the 17th-century religious wars to the 19th-century nationalist movements in Europe to the near extermination of the Jewish people under Nazi Germany—North Americans have struggled to learn how to respect each other's differences and live in harmony.

Millions of immigrants from scores of homelands brought diversity to our continent. In a mass migration, some 12 million immigrants passed through the waiting rooms of New York's Ellis Island; thousands more came to the West Coast. At first, these immigrants were welcomed because labor was needed to meet the demands of the Industrial Age. Soon, however, the new immigrants faced the prejudice of earlier immigrants who saw them as a burden on the economy. Legislation was passed to limit immigration. The Chinese Exclusion Act of 1882 was among the first laws closing the doors to the promise of America. The Japanese were also effectively excluded by this law. In 1924, Congress set immigration quotas on a country-by-country basis.

Such prejudices might have triggered war, as they did in Europe, but North Americans chose negotiation and compromise, instead. This determination to resolve differences peacefully has been the hallmark of the peoples of North America.

The remarkable ability of Americans to live together as one people was seriously threatened by the issue of slavery. It was a symptom of growing intolerance in the world. Thousands of settlers from the British Isles had arrived in the colonies as indentured servants, agreeing to work for a specified number of years on farms or as apprentices in return for passage to America and room and board. When the first Africans arrived in the then-British colonies during the 17th century, some colonists thought that they too should be treated as indentured servants. Eventually, the question of whether the Africans should be viewed as indentured, like the English, or as slaves who could be owned for life, was considered in a Maryland court. The court's calamitous decree held that blacks were slaves bound to lifelong servitude, and so were their children.

America went through a time of moral examination and civil war before it finally freed African slaves and their descendants. The principle that all people are created equal had faced its greatest challenge and survived.

Yet the court ruling that set blacks apart from other races fanned flames of discrimination that burned long after slavery was abolished—and that still flicker today. The concept of racism had existed for centuries in countries throughout the world. For instance, when the Manchus conquered China in the 13th century, they decreed that Chinese and Manchus could not intermarry. To impress their superiority on the conquered Chinese, the Manchus ordered all Chinese men to wear their hair in a long braid called a queue.

By the 19th century, some intellectuals took up the banner of racism, citing Charles Darwin. Darwin's scientific studies hypothesized that highly evolved animals were dominant over other animals. Some advocates of this theory applied it to humans, asserting that certain races were more highly evolved than others and thus were superior.

This philosophy served as the basis for a new form of discrimination, not only against nonwhite people but also against various ethnic groups. Asians faced harsh discrimination and were depicted by popular 19th-century newspaper cartoonists as depraved, degenerate, and deficient in intelligence. When the Irish flooded American cities to escape the famine in Ireland, the cartoonists caricatured the typical "Paddy" (a common term for Irish immigrants) as an apelike creature with jutting jaw and sloping forehead.

By the 20th century, racism and ethnic prejudice had given rise to virulent theories of a Northern European master race. When Adolf Hitler came to power in Germany in 1933, he popularized the notion of Aryan supremacy. "Aryan," a term referring to the Indo-European races, was applied to so-called superior physical characteristics such as blond hair, blue eyes, and delicate facial features. Anyone with darker and heavier features was considered inferior. Buttressed by these theories, the German Nazi state from

1933 to 1945 set out to destroy European Jews, along with Poles, Russians, and other groups considered inferior. It nearly succeeded. Millions of these people were exterminated.

The tragedies brought on by ethnic and racial intolerance throughout the world demonstrate the importance of North America's efforts to create a society free of prejudice and inequality.

A relatively recent example of the New World's desire to resolve ethnic friction nonviolently is the solution the Canadians found to a conflict between two ethnic groups. A long-standing dispute as to whether Canadian culture was properly English or French resurfaced in the mid-1960s, dividing the peoples of the French-speaking Quebec Province from those of the English-speaking provinces. Relations grew tense, then bitter, then violent. The Royal Commission on Bilingualism and Biculturalism was established to study the growing crisis and to propose measures to ease the tensions. As a result of the commission's recommendations, all official documents and statements from the national government's capital at Ottawa are now issued in both French and English, and bilingual education is encouraged.

The year 1980 marked a coming of age for the United States's ethnic heritage. For the first time, the U.S. Census asked people about their ethnic background. Americans chose from more than 100 groups, including French Basque, Spanish Basque, French Canadian, Afro-American, Peruvian, Armenian, Chinese, and Japanese. The ethnic group with the largest response was English (49.6 million). More than 100 million Americans claimed ancestors from the British Isles, which includes England, Ireland, Wales, and Scotland. There were almost as many Germans (49.2 million) as English. The Irish-American population (40.2 million) was third, but the next largest ethnic group, the Afro-Americans, was a distant fourth (21 million). There was a sizable group of French ancestry (13 million), as well as of Italian (12 million). Poles, Dutch, Swedes, Norwegians, and Russians followed. These groups, and other smaller ones, represent the wondrous profusion of ethnic influences in North America.

Canada, too, has learned more about the diversity of its population. Studies conducted during the French/English conflict showed that Canadians were descended from Ukrainians, Germans, Italians, Chinese, Japanese, native Indians, and Eskimos, among others. Canada found it had no ethnic majority, although nearly half of its immigrant population had come from the British Isles. Canada, like the United States, is a land of immigrants for whom mutual tolerance is a matter of reason as well as principle.

The people of North America are the descendants of one of the greatest migrations in history. And that migration is not over. Koreans, Vietnamese, Nicaraguans, Cubans, and many others are heading for the shores of North America in large numbers. This mix of cultures shapes every aspect of our lives. To understand ourselves, we must know something about our diverse ethnic ancestry. Nothing so defines the North American nations as the motto on the Great Seal of the United States: *E Pluribus Unum*—Out of Many, One. ✍

Many Slovak Americans still celebrate special occasions such as weddings with traditional dress, dance, and music.

FROM FARM TO FACTORY

Since they first began arriving in North America during the 1870s, Slovak immigrants have played a significant role in the development of the United States and Canada. As factory workers, coal miners, and dockhands, immigrants from rural Slovakia helped fuel the industrial revolution in the United States. Later, intellectuals and political refugees made their mark, particularly in Canada. Many descendants of Slovak immigrants now make their livings as lawyers, doctors, teachers, and business people.

In the late 19th and early 20th centuries, approximately 650,000 Slovaks emigrated to the United States and Canada. Most of those who came to the United States arrived before World War I, and in Canada between World War I and World War II. After World War II a smaller wave of immigrants, mostly intellectuals and political refugees, landed in North America. Some of the Slovak immigrants returned to the old country after saving enough money to buy land there, but most—about 500,000—settled in the New World for good. Today, between 1 and 2 million Americans and about 40,000 Canadians claim Slovak ancestry.

Once they arrived in the New World, Slovak immigrants struggled to make a place for themselves in American and Canadian society. They founded churches where they could worship in their own language; schools where their children could learn Slovak language, culture, and the tenets of their faith; newspapers that reported on the immigrant community as well as on events in the old country; and fraternal and civic societies that bettered their economic and political lot.

Most Slovak Americans still live in the northeastern and midwestern parts of the country—about half in Pennsylvania and the remainder in Connecticut, Illinois, Indiana, Michigan, New Jersey, New York, and Ohio—where the majority of Slovak immigrants originally settled. Canadian Slovaks are concentrated in the provinces of Ontario and Quebec, particularly around the cities of Toronto and Montreal. The aging first and second generations still live in their old ethnic neighborhoods near the mines and mills where they worked and built their parish churches. The more affluent third and fourth generations, however, have moved to the suburbs.

Today, Slovaks in the United States and Canada have reached a crossroads. Although many people of Slovak descent carry on the rich religious and cultural traditions of their forebears, the younger generations have been thoroughly assimilated into the society around them. Assimilation has allowed some to make a broader mark on American or Canadian society and culture; a number of prominent figures in business, science, art, literature, history, theology, sports, and entertainment are either Slovak-born or of Slovak descent. Slovaks have found success in the New World, but many older Slovaks fear that assimilation may have a harmful effect on the vitality of Slovak ethnicity.

Regionalism, class differences, religion, and language made the Slovaks a diverse group of immigrants. The vast majority of Slovaks who came to North America had been rural farmers or manual laborers, and they practiced various folk cultures specific to their regions of origin. Those who came after World War II often had more education, had lived in cities, and identified with western European culture. In addition, the Slovaks practiced a variety of religions. Most were Roman Catholic, but a significant number were Lutheran, and smaller groups practiced either Greek Catholicism or Calvinism. Finally, not all Slovaks spoke exactly the same language; the country's western, central, and eastern regions each had distinct dialects.

The differences between the various groups of Slovak immigrants initially divided them in America as they had in Europe. Not until they began to assimilate into the culture of their new homeland did newcomers consider themselves members of the same ethnic group. Many Slovaks had traveled to the New World with others from their village or region who shared the same religious beliefs and language; and when they arrived, they often settled together, joining established communities of immigrants like themselves. In this way, Slovak immigrants tended to preserve their regional identity. As they learned to speak English, however, their regionalism faded, and members of different Slovak groups began to share a common Slovak heritage.

Slovak immigrants fled crushing poverty in their rural homeland to work in thriving New World industries.

In the 10th century, Hungarian Magyars took possession of lands that later became known as Slovakia.

A BRIEF HISTORY OF SLOVAKIA

The Slovaks are a small nation of Slavic people who live in the heart of central Europe. Bordered by Poland, the Soviet Union, Hungary, and Austria, Slovakia occupies the eastern portion of present-day Czechoslovakia. The Carpathian Mountains, covered with vast forests, make up most of the region's landscape. The lowlands to the south have always supported agriculture, but industry now dominates the Slovak economy. More than 4 million Slovaks— 30 percent of Czechoslovakia's population—live there today, many in the capital city of Bratislava, a port on the Danube River.

For the last 1,100 years the Slovaks have struggled to preserve their identity in the face of foreign domination. Only twice in its history has Slovakia enjoyed independence, and then only for very short periods of time. Foreign rule has been responsible for dividing the Slovaks into three religious denominations, and each religious sect has distanced itself from the others. This division has made it difficult for the Slovaks to unite against their common enemies to regain independence, but throughout their history the people have successfully resisted the attempts of their conquerors to eradicate Slovak culture.

Early Independence

Slovakia traces its history back to the 5th century, when ancestors of the modern Slovaks settled in the region that would later be known as Slovakia. By the 9th century, about A.D. 830, these early Slovaks, together with their Moravian neighbors, had established a state called Great Moravia.

In A.D. 863, the Apostles of the Slavs—Saints Cyril and Methodius—brought Byzantine Christianity (Greek Catholicism) to the area. The Great Moravian Empire eventually grew to include all of present-day Czechoslovakia (the regions of Slovakia, Moravia, and Bohemia), southern Poland, and northern Hungary.

Great Moravia did not last long, however. There was a powerful threat to the west—the Holy Roman Empire. This empire, in the area that is now Germany, had emerged from the remains of another empire established in A.D. 800 by Charlemagne. Charlemagne's holdings initially encompassed much of western and central Europe, but his successors split it into three parts, and the German portion took the name Holy Roman Empire. In the 10th century, the Germans joined with the Hungarians to the east, attacked Great Moravia, and destroyed it.

Religious Upheaval

After conquering Great Moravia, the Holy Roman Empire claimed Bohemia and Moravia, while the kingdom of Hungary annexed Slovakia. The Hungarians forced the Slovaks to convert to Roman Catholicism and at first suppressed economic and social development in the region, but they allowed the people to retain their language and culture. In the 13th century, when Tartar invasions weakened Hungary, economic conditions improved for Slovakia. Over the course of the next 600 years, the Slovaks and Hungarians adopted elements of each other's way of life; and by the end of the 18th century, the two groups had become thoroughly integrated.

The emperor of the Holy Roman Empire, which annexed the Czech regions of Bohemia and Moravia, wore a crown depicting biblical King Solomon.

In the 12th century, Greek Catholicism began to return to Slovakia via Rusin (Ruthenian) shepherds who crossed the Carpathian Mountains. The process of religious diversification continued with the advent of the Protestant Reformation in the 16th century. Triggered by Martin Luther's criticism of Roman Catholic doctrine and the authority of the centralized church, the Reformation swept through most of Europe, including Hungary. Almost all Slovaks immediately adopted Lutheranism.

After suffering so many defections from its ranks, the Roman Catholic church sought to recapture as many of its former members as possible. It launched the Counter-Reformation in the 17th century and succeeded in regaining the allegiance of most Slovaks. Some remained Lutherans, while a tiny percentage adopted Calvinism, another form of Protestantism.

A small number of Slovak Protestants who rejected reconversion to Roman Catholicism converted instead to Greek Catholicism. The Greek Catholic church had gained recognition from Rome as a legitimate church, so its members were not subject to Roman Catholic attempts to convert them. The new converts added their numbers to those who had become Greek Catholics earlier by intermarrying with the Rusins. By the

Francis Joseph ascended to the throne of Hungary in 1867, when the dual monarchy of Austria-Hungary was formed.

Martin Luther sparked the Protestant Reformation of the 16th century with his censure of the Roman Catholic church.

end of the Counter-Reformation in the 18th century, approximately 80 percent of the Slovaks had returned to Roman Catholicism, 15 percent remained Lutherans, some smaller groups practiced Greek Catholicism, others, Calvinism. A small community of non-Slovak Jews had by that time settled in Slovakia as well.

The division of the Slovaks by religion fostered differences in language as well. Slovak Lutherans, like other Protestants, wanted to conduct church services in their native tongues rather than in Latin, the language used by Roman Catholics. But for reasons of simplicity, the Lutherans decided on Czech as their uniform liturgical language. Slovak dialects share many similarities with the Greek language, which had been codified in the 15th century, but there were as yet no established rules of grammar and spelling for the Slovak language used by most Slovak Lutherans. Byzantine Catholics worshiped in Church Slavonic, and the Calvinists started using their own eastern Slovak dialect in the 18th century.

Poverty and National Oppression in Hungary

As the Counter-Reformation drew to a close, two changes in the Slovak way of life led to a population explosion. At the same time that an improvement in hygiene caused a dramatic decline in Slovak mortality, a change in diet helped fuel the rapid growth of the Slovak population.

For centuries, the Slovaks had subsisted on meager crops of wheat grown in the few lowlands. This limited food supply had restricted the size of the population. But when the potato was imported from the New World in the 18th century, it thrived in mountainous Slovakia and increased the quantity of food available to the people. In addition, scientists had by then demonstrated the connection between dirt and disease. Europeans began to pay more attention to the quality of the water they drank and to wash more often. As a result, the Slovak population doubled from 1.1 million in 1720 to over 2.4 million in 1840. The four eastern counties of Slovakia—Spis, Saris, Zemplin, and Abov—saw the most dramatic growth: The population there increased sevenfold.

At the start of the 16th century, the Habsburg Dynasty of Austria moved to attach Hungary to the Austrian Empire, beginning with Slovakia. Until 1848, when the Hungarian revolution took place, the Austrian Empire was a feudal society. Nobles, who owned land, forced serfs to cultivate it. Feudal lords kept the crops from most of their land for their own use, allocating only small portions of land for the serfs to raise their own crops on. In payment for the use of these plots, serfs annually turned over to their lords a portion of their own crop. Although the lords did not actually own the serfs, they could not leave their land without the permission of their lords. Nevertheless, in the 18th and early 19th centuries, more than 200,000 Slovak serfs managed to escape, fleeing to the Banat and Backa regions of present-day Yugoslavia. Those who stayed behind continued to live in poverty and oppression.

Not all Slovaks were serfs, however. Some had acquired land and had integrated into Hungarian society to such an extent that the Hungarians had granted them the status of nobility. The Hungarian and Slovak nobility often intermarried, and they shared certain tastes common to the cosmopolitan European culture of the time. Slovak nobles read the same books as other European nobles, enjoyed the same classical music, ate the same cuisine, and dressed similarly. Among themselves they might speak Slovak dialects, but they could also communicate in Latin, the official language of the kingdom of Hungary until 1840.

But the integration of Slovak and Hungarian culture was short-lived. Nationalism—the idea that nations and ethnic groups should retain their own language, customs, and culture—swept through Europe, reaching Hungary in the 1780s. Inspired by nationalism, the Slovaks sought to preserve their ethnic identity at all costs, even though many regional, religious, linguistic, and class differences threatened the unity of Slovak culture.

For much of its history, Slovakia was part of the Austro-Hungarian Empire ruled by the Habsburgs. Joseph II, who ruled the empire from 1780 to 1790, sits alongside his brother and successor, Leopold II.

Slovak and Czech immigrants served in the American army during World War I, hoping to free their homeland from the oppressive Austro-Hungarian Empire.

At the same time, Emperor Joseph II of Austria tried to introduce German as the official language of his empire, which now included the kingdom of Hungary. The Hungarian nobility rebelled and campaigned for the use of their native language, Magyar, rather than Latin or German, in Hungarian schools, government, and commerce. By 1840 Magyar had become the official language of the kingdom of Hungary. The nobility then attempted to force everyone in Hungary—even people of non-Hungarian nationalities, such as the Slovaks, Germans, Rusins, Romanians, Serbs, and Croats—to learn it, in order to unify the culture.

The Hungarian and Austrian efforts to establish official languages fueled a revival of Slovak national pride. Slovak intellectuals, rejecting the suggestion that Slovaks use Magyar as their official language, demanded instead that it be Slovak in the Slovak districts of Hungary. Other ethnic groups made similar arguments for their own languages. Each group systematized its own language and began to produce a literature in it.

In 1787 a Roman Catholic priest named Anton Bernolak codified the western Slovak dialect. Roman Catholic priests began to create a literature in this dialect, while Lutheran Slovaks continued writing in ancient Czech. Later, in response to the establishment of Magyar as the official language of Hungary, Ludovit Stur, a Slovak patriot, joined the battle. He believed that in order for the Slovaks to unite against the Magyar threat of assimilation, they needed to share one standard dialect. Because most eastern Slovaks had trouble understanding Czech and western Slovak, Stur suggested that central Slovak be the standard, used by everyone. He codified that dialect in 1843, and in 1851 the Slovak Roman Catholics adopted it. Central Slovak became the common literary language of Slovak intellectuals, although most people continued to use their local dialects in everyday speech.

In 1845 Stur started publishing the first Slovak-language periodical, *Slovenskje Narodnje Novini*, inspiring a small group of Slovak intellectuals to publish newspapers, almanacs, novels, and poetry in their own tongue. The Hungarian government, of course, opposed such efforts at unifying the Slovak people and fought the nationalists for the allegiance of the Slovak masses. During this time some Slovaks went over to the Hungarian side. A famous example was poet Alexander Petrovic (1823–1849), who changed his name to the Hungarian Sandor Petofi and went on to play a major role in the Hungarian revolution of 1848. Others, such as poet Pavol Orszagh Hviezdoslav (1849–1921), remained loyal to the Slovak cause. He composed his early works in Magyar but later returned to his roots and became one of the great Slovak poets. The Slovaks' struggle to retain their own language and culture persisted until 1918, when the new republic of Czecho-Slovakia was formed and Slovak culture allowed to thrive, unimpeded by official censure.

In 1848 Hungary revolted against Austrian domination. Although the effort failed, it led the rulers of the Austrian Empire to abolish serfdom. The serfs gained their freedom, but most ended up with less land to cultivate than they had held before liberation. Overpopulation and poverty continued, as did the emigration from Slovakia. Many former serfs went to work on the estates of Hungarian nobles in the south; others traveled to Austria, particularly Vienna, hoping to find industrial jobs; others ventured to Budapest, the booming Hungarian capital. Some wandered through western Europe as tinkers, earning a few pennies by sharpening and repairing scissors, knives, and other household implements.

The creation in 1867 of Austria-Hungary, a dual monarchy, gave the Hungarians more control over what was now their half of an empire. They redoubled their efforts to unify Hungary and grew even less tolerant of Slovak nationalism. In 1875 the government closed the *Matica Slovenska*, a cultural institution founded in 1863 to foster Slovak language and culture. At the same time, Hungary nationalized the three high schools controlled by the Slovaks as well as many of the 1,800 Slovak parochial grade schools.

The Hungarian government, accusing Slovak newspaper editors and intellectuals of "inciting against the Magyar nationality," jailed and fined many of them. In cooperation with the Roman Catholic hierarchy of Hungary, which supported the assimilation of non-Magyar nationalities, the government transferred Slovak nationalist clergy to non-Slovak parishes. But even though the Hungarians defeated the Slovak intellectuals on some fronts, they did not succeed in assimilating the people as a whole. In the face of political oppression and discrimination, Slovak nationalism strengthened.

As conditions in Europe worsened, Slovak immigration to the New World began. Between 1870 and 1914, more than 650,000 Slovaks came to the United States and Canada. The freedom they found there encouraged nationalist Slovak immigrants to agitate on behalf of Slovaks in Hungary. American Slovak nationalists sent money to beleaguered newspaper editors and writers in Slovakia, who used it to help finance election campaigns in Hungary.

The Creation of Czechoslovakia

During World War I Slovak patriots worked toward liberation by assisting in the defeat of the Austro-Hungarian Empire. Immigrants in the New World, hoping to liberate those still living in Slovakia from oppressive Hungarian rule, offered their help. They joined forces with Czech immigrants who sought Czech independence from the Austrian half of the empire. Czech and Slovak leaders signed the Cleveland Agreement (1915) and Pittsburgh Agreement (1918), in which they pledged to fight Austria-Hungary by supporting the Al-

The Pittsburgh Agreement, signed by many prominent Slovak and Czech Americans, declared the immigrants' support for the creation of an independent Czecho-Slovak state.

Tomas Masaryk, Czech leader of the wartime Czecho-Slovak independence movement, became the first president of the new republic.

lies (chiefly France, Britain, Russia, and the United States) with soldiers and money.

The two agreements also introduced the idea of an independent Czecho-Slovak state. The patriots hoped that if the Allies defeated the Central Powers (Germany and Austria-Hungary), the Czechs and Slovaks would be permitted to create a new federated state, Czecho-Slovakia. According to the Cleveland and Pittsburgh agreements, the Czechs and Slovaks were to have equal roles in governing Czecho-Slovakia. The Slovaks who signed the agreements championed "home rule": an autonomous Slovak government with its own courts and administration.

The Allies won the war in 1918, and on October 28 of that year the Czechs and Slovaks gained their own republic, with Czech professor T. G. Masaryk as its first president. No sooner was Czecho-Slovakia established, however, than the Slovaks were disappointed again. Although Masaryk had led the wartime struggle for independence and drafted and signed the Pittsburgh Agreement, which had provided for Slovak home rule, he repudiated the agreement when he returned to his homeland from exile in the West. With the support of a Czech majority and a small number of Slovaks, he and the new Czecho-Slovak Parliament created a unitary Czechoslovakia in 1920.

Because the Czechs outnumbered the Slovaks by more than two to one, and because Czechoslovakia, a parliamentary democracy, granted each citizen one vote, the Czechs easily denied Slovak demands for equality. Masaryk and his followers expected the Slovaks to give up their language and culture and to merge with the Czechs to become a new ethnic group that would call itself "Czechoslovak." Most Slovaks rejected this course of action and continued to clamor for the implementation of the Cleveland and Pittsburgh pacts. The Reverend Andrej Hlinka, then head of the Slovak People's party, and Jozef Tiso, another influential figure, led the ensuing 20-year struggle for Slovak home rule.

The Munich Agreement of 1938 brought the Slovaks a step closer to autonomy. The agreement—between England and France on the one hand, and Germany on the other—severely weakened the Czechoslovak state. Germany's Nazi chancellor, Adolf Hitler, took possession of most of the Sudetenland, a German-speaking part of Czechoslovakia. The Czechs subsequently granted the Slovaks home rule. The new arrangement, under which the Slovaks elected their own parliament, satisfied most of the Slovaks who had sought autonomy.

Hitler, however, hoped to reestablish the German Holy Roman Empire that had ruled Bohemia and Moravia for almost a thousand years. He decided to annex the Czech regions but worried that Hungary and Poland would divide Slovakia between them if he took the Czech lands. On March 13, 1939, he summoned Monsignor Jozef Tiso, the prime minister of Slovakia, to Berlin and gave him an ultimatum: If Tiso did not declare Slovak independence from Czechoslovakia, Hitler would not protect Slovakia from moves against it by Hungary or Poland.

The following day, Monsignor Tiso reported to the Slovak parliament on his meeting with Hitler, and the parliament declared Slovak independence. Hitler im-

Jozef Tiso headed a Nazi-controlled Slovak state during World War II.

From his office in London, exiled president Edvard Benes directed the activities of underground resisters working to overthrow Hitler's regime in Czechoslovakia.

mediately put the state under his protection, while German troops occupied Bohemia and Moravia. After 1,100 years of foreign rule, the Slovaks finally had their own state. Unfortunately, German domination was so strong that the Slovaks gained very little freedom or autonomy.

Edvard Benes, the last president of pre-Munich Czechoslovakia, fled to the West to establish a new liberation movement. Because Benes found little support in the West, he went to Moscow in 1943 and made an agreement with Joseph Stalin, the Communist party Secretary of the Soviet Union. Benes asked Stalin to help reunite the Czechs and Slovaks into a new Czechoslovakia after Hitler's defeat. In return, Benes would allow communists to participate in the postwar Czechoslovak government.

Despite rule by an authoritarian regime, most Slovaks supported their new republic. The minority that did not—Slovak Lutherans, communists, and liberals—protested the manner in which Slovakia had gained its independence. Their complaints multiplied when the government acquiesced to Hitler's requirement that Jews living in Slovakia be resettled in Poland. The Nazis, of course, were exterminating Jews in concentration camps in Poland. Once the Slovak government learned of the ultimate fate of the deported Jews, it halted the deportations. By then, however, more than half of Slovakia's Jews had been murdered.

In August 1944, assisted by Soviet guerrilla fighters who had parachuted into Slovak territory, the various dissident groups revolted against the Germans and the Slovak state. Within six weeks, the German army had crushed the uprising, and until May 1945 Slovakia served as a battleground for the conflict between the German and Soviet armies.

Communism

When the Soviet Red Army drove the Germans out of Slovakia in May 1945, Stalin kept his promise to Benes. Czechoslovakia reformed, with Benes as president. Benes kept his part of the bargain, allowing Czech and Slovak communists to assume various roles in the government. In 1948, after violence, mass arrests, and the execution of Tiso, the communists seized control of the Czechoslovak government. Czechoslovakia became a communist state controlled by Moscow.

Despite the popularity of liberal president Alexander Dubcek, the Soviets removed him as head of the Czechoslovak Communist party in 1968.

Once again the Slovaks had fallen under foreign rule. But they continued to demand the right to govern themselves as a nation separate from the Czechs. Some Slovak Communist party members paid for their insubordination at the notorious show trials of the early 1950s. At these trials, Czech leaders accused the Slovak Communists of "bourgeois nationalism"—a willingness to sacrifice the communist ideal of achieving a classless society in order to pursue their nationalist goals. One of the Slovak Communist leaders, Deputy Foreign Minister Vladimir Clementis, was executed. Gustav Husak, who has since become Communist party chief and president of Czechoslovakia, spent 10 years in prison.

In spite of Czech reprisals, communist and noncommunist Slovak nationalists persevered in their efforts. They finally triumphed when Alexander Dubcek, a Slovak leader, became party boss in 1967. Dubcek instituted a liberalization movement to make the government more democratic and in 1968 directed the rewriting of the Czechoslovak constitution to read, "We, the Czech and Slovak nations." The liberal government reorganized the country into a Czech Socialist Republic and a Slovak Socialist Republic, united into a Czecho-

Land-locked Slovakia occupies the eastern portion of present-day Czechoslovakia.

slovak Socialist Federation. In response to Dubcek's reforms, the Soviet Union and several of its Eastern European allies invaded Czechoslovakia in the summer of 1968.

The Soviets failed to suppress the liberalization, but they replaced Dubcek with Gustav Husak. The new party leader helped put the Czechoslovak government back under the control of the Communist party and the Soviet Union. Slovakia, however, retained its status as a republic. Today, Slovakia is still not a free and independent state, but Slovaks have finally received recognition as a distinct nation and obtained a measure of political autonomy in their homeland. ❧

Installed by Moscow after Dubcek's dismissal, Gustav Husak has governed Czechoslovakia in accordance with Soviet directives.

Immigrants arriving in Canada often journeyed westward to continue their farming lives in the New World.

ARRIVING IN THE NEW WORLD

The earliest Slovak immigrants left their homeland during the population explosion of the 18th century. Overcrowding led to even greater poverty than the Slovaks had suffered before, and at the same time the Hungarians intensified their efforts to suppress Slovak culture. Many Slovaks sought a better life in other European countries, and they eventually established colonies throughout central Europe, particularly in the cities.

Poor economic conditions coupled with political oppression prompted Slovak migration in the late 19th and early 20th centuries as well. Fully three quarters of all Slovaks who immigrated to the United States before World War I came from the counties of Spis, Saris, Zemplin, and Abov in eastern Slovakia, where poverty was at its worst because of the sevenfold increase in population over the course of 120 years. Slovak migration continued after World War I. During the period following World War II, thousands of political refugees fled persecution in Slovakia. Today, Slovaks still come to the New World for many of the same reasons that have brought them here since the 19th century.

In the late 1800s and early 1900s, Slovak immigrants looked across the sea for opportunity—to North and South America and as far away as Australia. They had

Slovak immigrants left behind lives of poverty in overpopulated villages.

heard of plentiful jobs and even of gold in the streets of America. Unemployed laborers in Slovakia would gather in local bars to hear the tales told by early travelers who had returned from the New World. Dressed in fancy clothes and buying drinks for everyone, those who had seen America told of coal mines where one could earn five times as much as in Hungary.

Although they were not to find gold in America's streets, Slovaks did find work there. When the United States began to industrialize in the 19th century, it needed workers willing to toil for low wages. Most of these workers had come from Ireland, but after 1865 the Irish started to organize labor unions that campaigned for better pay and more humane conditions. Unwilling to meet Irish demands, the industrialists investigated other sources of labor. They looked all over Europe and finally found willing workers in the Austro-Hungarian and Russian empires, where farmers and laborers lived in poverty, often deprived of their political rights by the imperial governments. The dissatisfied Slovaks offered an abundant supply of labor to American industry. Agents for railroad and coal mining companies initially lured about 5,000 Slovak laborers to America to work, paying their passage.

Young single men, hoping to make their fortunes in America before returning home, arrived first. They laid track for the railroads, mined coal in the anthracite and bituminous fields of Pennsylvania and Illinois, and labored in the thriving steel mills of the industrial Northeast and Midwest. For $1.50 a day, they usually worked 12-hour days, 7 days a week. Most of the workers lived in boardinghouses, where several workers, working different shifts and sleeping at different times, often shared a single bed.

These first Slovak laborers stayed in America an average of five years. Because they regarded their situation as temporary, and because their lives in Europe had been so miserable, the workers generally resigned themselves to the hardships of the New World. Living frugally, they usually managed within six months to repay the cost of their passage from Europe. Thereafter they saved their money, sending it home in hopes of buying land in the old country. Many shared the dream of returning to Slovakia to lead the good life on land of their own, whereas others planned to bring their relatives to America.

When they returned home to buy land, however, most found that they could no longer tolerate conditions there. Having grown accustomed to a life of relative prosperity and freedom, they could not readjust to the poverty and oppression they had almost forgotten. So they packed up their families and went back to America. In the end, only 20 percent of the Slovaks who left for America between 1870 and 1924 returned to Slovakia and stayed.

Throughout the 1880s and 1890s, and up until the outbreak of World War I, Slovaks poured into North America. Like millions of other immigrants from all over Europe, the Slovaks made the journey—which took anywhere from one to four weeks—by boat. Most immigrants traveled third class, or "steerage." Crammed into unventilated cargo holds unfit for human habitation, these passengers often had nothing to eat but herring supplied in barrels by the shipping company. Many immigrants never tasted even this meager fare, spending the entire trip confined to their bunks with seasickness.

Immigrants arriving in New York Harbor before 1892 had to pass through Castle Garden immigration station; those arriving afterward went through Ellis Island. At these immigration stations, officials checked their documentation and gave them medical exams to determine their fitness to enter the United States. Slovaks who passed inspection usually traveled on to the Slovak communities that had sprung up in the industrial regions of North America.

Some Slovak immigrants found America less than hospitable at first. When, for instance, 21-year-old Stefan Balsaj of Tulcik and seven of his friends landed in Philadelphia, Pennsylvania, in January of 1880, suspi-

Many of the earliest Slovak immigrants, young single men, toiled 12 hours a day in Pennsylvania coal mines.

When health and weather permitted, immigrants traveling in steerage came up on deck for a breath of fresh air.

cious city officials denied them entry to the city and forced them to leave. They walked to Trenton, New Jersey, to find work, but again they were turned away. Wrapped in blankets against the cold, they looked like undesirable vagabonds. Balsaj and his penniless friends wandered for three more days before a sympathetic Czech in South Bethlehem, Pennsylvania, took them in and found them jobs at the iron works there.

Settling In: Early Slovak Communities

Most Slovak immigrants came to the northeastern and midwestern states, settling in and around industrial cities such as Pittsburgh, Pennsylvania; Cleveland, Ohio; and Chicago, Illinois. They lived first in the poorest neighborhoods, often in areas abandoned by the increasingly prosperous Irish, and found jobs in the coal mines and steel mills where the Irish had worked for years. The Irish greeted the Slovaks with hostility, believing that the new immigrants would take away their jobs. In fact, the Slovaks actually opened the way for the Irish to move "upstairs" to better-paid supervisory posts, while Slovaks took over the less appealing tasks. Still, the earlier immigrants taunted the Slovak laborers with the nickname "Hunky," a crude slur against Hungary, their country of origin.

The first Slovaks to arrive in Canada came via the United States in the 1880s, seeking work in the mines of the Rocky Mountains of Alberta and British Columbia or in the industrial provinces of Ontario and Quebec. They settled in such places as Lethbridge and Blairmore, Alberta, and Fernie, British Columbia, where they mined coal and eventually established permanent communities. In the 1890s, others discovered that unlike the American West, the Canadian West still had plenty of unclaimed farmland. They went to farm in the rich prairie provinces of Manitoba and Saskatchewan, founding Hun's Valley and Esterhazy, Manitoba; Kenaston, Saskatchewan; and similar communities. Another group of Slovaks, mostly from the Orava region in north central Slovakia, made its home in the twin cities of Fort William and Port Arthur on Lake Superior. This urban area, now known as Thunder Bay, was an important Great Lakes port where the immigrants worked as stevedores, loading and unloading lake freighters and freight trains.

Slovaks arriving in the New World after the 1870s created communities that made life easier for them than it had been for the earlier arrivals. To supplement their families' incomes, married immigrants took boarders into the houses they rented from the mining and steel companies. Usually these boarders came from the same village or region in Slovakia, so the boardinghouses served as miniature versions of Old World communities. People who practiced the same religion, spoke the same dialect, and enjoyed the same food and music shared the simple quarters and felt a kinship that helped them survive harsh working conditions.

The first generation of American and Canadian Slovaks assimilated very little. They married fellow Slovaks almost exclusively. As in Europe, Slovaks in the New World had very large families, often with five or six children, and two or more generations lived under the same roof. Married children lived with their parents until they could afford a place of their own, and when they did move out, they usually did not go far.

Slovak industrial laborers led a hard life, working 12 hours a day for 12½ cents an hour. Every two weeks, when factory shifts changed, they toiled 24 hours straight. Workers began their days with breakfast at 5:30 A.M., then worked from 6:00 A.M. to noon, when

Boardinghouses provided food and shelter so cheaply that immigrants could save money to buy land back home.

they took half an hour for lunch. When the day shift ended at 6:00 P.M., they usually headed to a local Slovak saloon before making their way home to their families and boarders. A supper of soup, meat, and dumplings awaited them, followed by an evening of playing with the children or reading the paper. Others returned to the saloon.

Saloons were a tradition brought over from the old country. Slovak saloons sprang up in America to meet the immigrants' demand for places to gather and drink. These taverns joined the countless establishments catering to workers of various other nationalities that surrounded almost every mine, mill, refinery, or other place of work. Slovak saloons proliferated in the 1880s, eventually becoming community institutions where immigrants gathered not only to drink but also to catch up on the local gossip, trade tall tales, and discuss work or politics. Many saloons also served good meals at low prices and offered lodging upstairs.

As proprietors of the community's social and political centers, many saloonkeepers became community leaders. Michael Bosak, for instance, ran a saloon in Oliphant, Pennsylvania, and later went on to become an influential banker, fraternal leader, and publisher. The importance of the saloon in immigrant life and the dedication of individuals like Bosak to community service reveals an attitude shared by many Slovak immigrants that the group was more important than the individual. In the New World, Slovaks formed close-knit communities that made the hardships of poverty more tolerable and gave some the encouragement they needed to pursue their dreams of a better life.

Three Immigrants' Stories: The New World Fulfills Its Promise

Nurtured by their communities, three Slovak immigrants in particular—Michael Bosak, Andrew Duda, and Stephen Roman—achieved the prosperity most immigrants hoped for. Yet even these highly successful

Although many lost their lives in the steel mills, unskilled Slovak laborers eagerly filled the plentiful jobs there.

Slovak immigrants did not forget their humble origins, as evidenced by their continued involvement in church, fraternal, and nationalist activities. All three returned to the community the support it had given them, easing the way for those who followed. Proof that the New World could fulfill its promise, their stories drew hundreds of thousands of Slovaks to North America.

In many ways typical of Slovaks who rushed to America, Bosak, Duda, and Roman shared the aspirations of all immigrants who set out for the golden land of opportunity. Slovak immigrants fled poverty and oppression in their homeland, some hoping for no more than a regular job and a steady paycheck, others dreaming of striking it rich and leading a life of ease and luxury. Although most immigrants never made it farther than the steel towns, they nonetheless found their life in America much kinder than the life they had known in Slovakia.

Born on December 10, 1869, Michael Bosak came from the village of Okruhle in Saris County, one of the poorest and most overpopulated regions of the old kingdom of Hungary. After four years of school, Michael joined his parents to work in the fields. Then, as a restless and ambitious 17–year-old, he heard about a better life in the United States. Without hesitating, he decided to go.

Bosak arrived in Hazleton, Pennsylvania, in 1886 and found his first job as a breaker boy in the coal mines, picking slate out of the coal through a grate, or "breaker," under his feet. Quickly tiring of coal mining and dissatisfied with his wage of 90 cents a day, he quit his job and drifted to other towns and other jobs, at one point working on the railroad. In 1891 he married and got a job delivering beer for a saloon in Freeland, Pennsylvania. Bosak saved his money, then moved to Oliphant in 1893 and opened his own saloon. In addition, he sold steamship tickets to immigrants returning to Slovakia.

His business prospered, and because he frequently deposited large sums into the First National Bank of

Saloons helped the Slovak immigrants forget the hardships of their daily lives.

Because of his ingenuity in attracting passengers for his steamships, as with this float promoting the sale of tickets to Europe, Michael Bosak became the first Slovak millionaire in America.

Oliphant, he was asked to become a director. He agreed and bought into the bank at the same time. By 1897 he held more stock than any other shareholder, and the board of directors elected him the bank's president. Still not satisfied, Bosak accumulated enough capital to open his own bank in Wilkes-Barre, Pennsylvania, in 1912, and in 1915 he opened the Bosak State Bank in Scranton, Pennsylvania.

Proud of his Slovak heritage, Bosak considered it important to contribute his skills, influence, and money toward bettering the lives of Slovak immigrants—and Slovaks still living in the old country. As longtime treasurer of the First Catholic Slovak Union (an organization committed to serving the Slovak community), he also participated in the World War I movement to liberate Slovakia. After the war, Bosak's national pride led him back to Slovakia. He opened a bank in Presov, the capital of his native Saris County, built a school in his hometown, Okruhle, and built a church in nearby Svidnik.

Bosak contributed further to the Slovak community as a newspaper publisher. In 1920 he bought the newspaper *Slovenska Obrana*, published in Scranton, Pennsylvania. One of the favorite Slovak-American newspapers among first- and second-generation immigrants from Slovakia, its presses did not stop rolling until 1972.

Bosak's saloonkeeping, banking, and publishing success made him the first Slovak millionaire in North America, as well as a hero to ambitious young Slovak immigrants. At the peak of his career, his business holdings totaled $15 million. But the 1919 passage of Prohibition by the United States Congress forced Bosak to close his saloon, weakening his business and destroying that of most other Slovak saloonkeepers.

Bosak might have stayed in business if not for the Great Depression. Unable to survive the 1929 stock market crash, Bosak's banks closed in 1931. Like so many others ruined by the depression, Bosak never recovered from his loss. His vast holdings were only a memory when he died on February 18, 1937. Despite its sad ending, Bosak's story proved that some Slovaks could achieve their dreams in America, and, indeed, that they had already begun to do so by the early years of the 20th century.

Better luck came to Andrew Duda, who was born on November 9, 1873, in the village of Velcice, Trencin County, Slovakia. One of ten children, Duda immigrated to the United States in 1909 in search of a better future. He settled in Cleveland, where he worked for three years in various factories. In 1912, Jan Pankuch, a local editor and fraternalist, established a Slovak-Lutheran retirement community, Slavia, in Florida. Duda moved to Florida to help organize Slavia and helped found Saint Luke's Lutheran congregation there, but he soon went bankrupt.

Returning to Cleveland, he carefully saved his money and planned another real-estate venture. In 1926 he had accumulated enough capital to buy a few hundred swampy acres in Florida. He and his three sons learned how to grow celery on their land, and their farm prospered. By plowing their profits back into the business, they were able to buy more land and expand their agricultural efforts to include radishes and citrus fruit. A longtime supporter of the church and retirement home he helped create, Duda donated 40 acres of land to Slavia, by that time renamed Lutheran Haven.

When he died on January 20, 1958, Duda owned 65,000 acres of Florida farmland and was a millionaire many times over. His sons later increased these holdings to 115,000 acres and leased 184,000 acres of rangeland in Australia. By 1986 the family's estimated net worth topped $450 million. The Slavia retirement home, recently renamed Oviedo, remains a vital Slovak-Lutheran community, much to the credit of Andrew Duda and his family. Duda exemplified the American dream that inspired so many Slovaks to leave their homes for the promised land. He also remained true to his Slovak heritage, making an indelible mark on the Slovak-American community.

Canada fulfilled its promise to many Slovak immigrants as well. One of the most notable successes there is Stephen B. Roman. Born on April 17, 1921, in Velky Ruskov, Zemplin County, Slovakia, Roman dropped out of high school in 1937 and came to Canada. He found his first job picking tomatoes in the vicinity of Oshawa, Ontario; he later worked for General Motors, and in 1942 he joined the Canadian army.

After his discharge in 1943, Roman tried his hand at stock-market speculation and made a $10,000 profit. He then took up prospecting. He struck oil in North Dakota, sold his oil well in 1953, and bought 900,000 shares of stock in North Denison uranium mines and gained an interest in the nearby Algoma uranium mine in northern Ontario.

Roman's purchases, which he later consolidated and renamed Denison Mines Limited, gave him control of the largest uranium mine in the world. He later diversified his holdings and tried to sell Denison Mines to an American company, but the Canadian prime minister blocked the sale. Roman sued but lost the case. His businesses continued to thrive, however, and his net worth is now estimated to exceed $200 million.

Andrew Duda's sons have ensured the continuing prosperity of their father's legacy, the Oviedo Lutheran retirement community.

Stephen Roman made his fortune in Canada and today serves as president of the Slovak World Congress, headquartered in Toronto, Ontario.

Roman also got involved in the political and religious life of Canadian Slovaks. As a Conservative party candidate, he ran twice for election to the Canadian Parliament, though he lost both times. A devout Greek Catholic, he fostered the career of his friend and pastor, the Reverend Michael Rusnak. In part because of Roman's efforts, the pope named Rusnak the eparch (bishop) of all Slovak Greek Catholics in Canada. Roman was also a Slovak nationalist who hoped to alert the world to the sad plight of Slovaks behind the Iron Curtain. For this purpose, he established the Slovak World Congress in 1970. Elected president of the congress at its founding, Roman still serves in that capacity today.

Michael Bosak, Andrew Duda, and Stephen Roman stand as examples of how the New World could fulfill its promise to some of the millions of immigrants of all nationalities arriving on its shores. These three immigrants, though, were first and foremost Slovaks to whom community success mattered no less than individual success. This ideal infused early Slovak immigrants, almost all of whom maintained ties to one or more religious, social, cultural, or political institutions. From the first days of Slovak immigration, fraternal benefit societies and the church have played particularly important roles in the experience of the Slovak community in North America. ⤜

Devoutly religious, Slovak immigrants established churches in their new communities as soon as they could.

THE COMMUNITY GROWS

Once the Slovaks had established themselves firmly on North American soil and their communities had begun to grow, their families, boardinghouses, and saloons no longer met all their social needs. Immigrants thus founded numerous civic and religious institutions, the most important of which were fraternal benefit organizations and churches. The original goals of these institutions included the preservation of Slovak religious and cultural life and also the improvement of conditions for Slovak immigrants and Slovaks still living in Europe.

Helping Themselves: Slovak Fraternal Organizations

Slovak fraternal benefit societies lent formal structure to the immigrants' lives and provided a means by which to stem the tide of assimilation. Many of the early immigrants wanted to preserve their native culture, and Slovak organizations helped maintain a distinct Slovak identity in North America. But by easing the immigrants' adjustment to the New World, fraternals ultimately encouraged assimilation.

ZA BOHA A NÁROD

BANKETTOM
K Pocte 41 Novoprijatych
CLENOV

Fraternal organizations sprang up across the continent to meet the social and civic needs of the immigrants.

Because the first Slovak immigrants landed in an America devoid of a welfare system, fraternal organizations frequently provided disability insurance and death benefits to workers and their families. When workers received injuries, lost limbs, or even died on the job, few employers and no government agencies paid their families any compensation. The fraternal benefit societies sought to fulfill this need. At monthly lodge meetings, they elected officers to oversee operations, collected dues from members, and discussed working conditions, life in America, and other crucial issues. They deposited their dues in treasuries, from which they paid out benefits to needy members.

Fraternal activities also helped immigrants adjust to American and Canadian ways. By electing officers, debating at meetings, and taking up collections to pay out benefits, lodge members learned the rudiments of democracy. Those who won lodge offices and presided over lodge debates sometimes graduated into local politics, while members with a journalistic bent found plenty of opportunity with the newspapers that the fraternals published. After tasting this freedom to govern themselves, most Slovak immigrants lost all desire to return to oppression in Hungary.

For the most part, fraternal benefit societies established membership on the basis of religious denomination. Roman Catholic, Greek Catholic, Lutheran, and Calvinist Slovaks set up their own organizations, sometimes within the same community. Many of these helped establish local church parishes and maintained an ongoing relationship with the church. Catholics often cemented this bond by naming the churches they built for the patron saints of their fraternals. Slovak immigrants also set up nondenominational organizations to further their nationalist aspiration of winning political independence for Slovakia.

By 1890, Slovaks had founded more than 40 fraternals throughout the northeastern and midwestern United States. A movement was born to transform the Slovak fraternal system from a scattering of small local lodges into a collection of organizations capable of acting on a nationwide basis. Peter V. Rovnianek, Slovak-American journalist and nationalist, led this movement. Rovnianek dreamed of a national fraternal organization that would not only be more effective in preserving Slovak culture and bettering Slovak life in America, but could also make a real contribution to the fight against the oppression of Slovaks in Hungary. His dedication to this ideal made Rovnianek one of the great leaders of the early Slovak-American community.

Peter V. Rovnianek hoped that a national federation of Slovak fraternal societies would help Slovakia win freedom from Hungary.

Born on June 27, 1867, in Dolny Hricov, Trencin County, Slovakia, Rovnianek went to Budapest, Hungary, to study for the Roman Catholic priesthood. As he studied, his pride in his Slovak heritage grew, but at that time the Hungarian government kept a close watch on the priesthood in an effort to suppress Slovak ethnic movements. Because nationalist Slovak priests often passed along their ideas to their congregations, the Hungarians singled them out as potential troublemakers. An avowed nationalist, Rovnianek was expelled from the seminary.

In 1888 he left Europe for Cleveland, Ohio, where he enrolled in the local seminary. His interest in Slovak

Like many Slovak Americans, the Reverend Stefan Furdek believed that fraternal organizations best served their members in conjunction with the church.

nationalism outweighed his desire to be a priest, however, and he never sought ordination. Instead, Rovnianek went on to become a prominent journalist, reporting on, among other things, the activities of the multiplying Slovak fraternal benefit societies.

After observing the fraternals, Rovnianek came to the conclusion that a national federation of fraternal organizations might help local societies achieve their aims. He led a small group of leaders in founding the National Slovak Society on February 15, 1890. This society hoped to recruit local Slovak fraternals from across America, with the goal of forming a single union with a central treasury and a coherent set of objectives.

As he organized the National Slovak Society, however, Rovnianek did not foresee the difficulties such a union would have because of the religious divisions within the Slovak community. He was dismayed when, a few months later, the Reverend Stefan Furdek of Cleveland opposed the nondenominational national fraternal. Furdek feared that without the guidance of Roman Catholic priests, such an organization would take an anticlerical (antipriest) stance. He pointed to the example of the Czech Slavic Benevolent Society headquartered in St. Louis, which had, in fact, rejected church involvement in fraternal activities.

Furdek and Rovnianek had first met at the Cleveland seminary where both had studied. Although they shared many interests and had an equal love for the Slovak people, they took different approaches to the concerns of Slovak Americans, and their lives ultimately followed very different routes.

Born in Trstena, county Orava, Slovakia, on September 2, 1855, Stefan Furdek came to the United States in 1882 to complete his studies for the Roman Catholic priesthood. He enrolled in the Seminary of the Diocese of Cleveland, where he was later ordained. Although assigned to a Czech parish in Cleveland (Slovaks had, as yet, no parish of their own in the United States), Furdek devoted much of his energy to Slovak immi-

(continued on page 57)

A SLOVAK AMERICAN FAMILY

HOLY
TRINITY
ROMAN
CATHOLIC
SLOVAK
CHURCH
1899 – 1902 – 1912

Even as they adopt New World customs, Slovak Americans retain their traditional commitment to family and church. Slovak-American newspapers also mix the old with the new, printing one section in English and another in Slovak.

The availability of education in North America has opened new job opportunities to Slovak Americans, many of whom pursue advanced degrees and professional careers rather than work in the mines and factories where their immigrant forebears labored.

Although traditional holiday celebrations have been modified by recent generations of Slovak Americans, on special occasions many families feast on such ethnic dishes as soups, sausages, and pastries.

Many Slovak-American families enjoy suburban comforts in communities such as Parma, Ohio; Columbus Heights, Minnesota; and Bethlehem, Pennsylvania.

(continued from page 48)

grants arriving in that city. In 1888 he helped Slovak Roman Catholics establish one of their first American parishes, Saint Ladislaus, in Cleveland.

Furdek combined his religious and civic interests through his involvement in Slovak fraternal life. When his rival Peter Rovnianek set up the National Slovak Society in 1890, Furdek countered by instituting the First Catholic Slovak Union, and when Rovnianek in 1891 helped found Zivena, a women's organization, Furdek organized the First Catholic Slovak Ladies Union in 1892. By appealing to the devout Roman Catholic Slovak majority, the fraternals established by Furdek became the two largest Slovak fraternal benefit societies in the world. Furdek also cofounded the literary society Matica Slovenska v Amerike in 1893, and in 1907 set up the Slovak League of America, a network organization for all Slovak-American societies.

Because of the efforts of leaders such as Rovnianek and Furdek, the last years of the 19th century saw a tremendous proliferation of fraternal benefit societies. Organizations sprang up to serve a wide variety of interests. In 1892 Lutherans founded the Slovak Evangelical Union, and in 1901 Calvinists formed their own Slovak Calvin Presbyterian Union. Slovak women, excluded from men's fraternals, set up their own societies, including some dedicated to the practice of gymnastics.

Dozens of societies throughout Canada and the United States modeled themselves after these flagship groups, but some militant nationalists grew dissatisfied with the social and civic bent of most fraternals. In 1896 a group of them established the Slovak Gymnastic Union Sokol in New York City. The members of this fraternal sought to attain physical fitness through gymnastics, in preparation for what they considered an inevitable war against the Hungarians. The union's Roman Catholic members, though, became uncomfortable when some of the group's leaders began expressing anticlerical ideas. They broke away in 1905, establishing the Slovak Catholic Sokol, a rival organization that eventually outgrew its model.

Members of the Slovak Gymnastic Union Sokol dedicated themselves to physical fitness in anticipation of war with Hungary.

Fraternal lodges helped Slovak immigrants maintain a sense of community and cope with life in the New World, but the sheer number of organizations tended to splinter the Slovaks into smaller, and often competing, groups. This division reflected the religious differences among the immigrants, the legacy of a history of domination by foreigners that had fragmented Slovakia into four major Christian denominations. Slovak immigrants carried their beliefs with them to the New World, so their communities in North America reflected the same denominational divisions that had characterized their homeland.

New World Churches

Despite their diverse affiliations, Slovak immigrants shared a common devotion to the church. As soon as their numbers were sufficient to support parishes, they built churches and found Slovak priests and ministers to teach their congregations. Religion colored almost every aspect of the workings of Slovak communities, from family life to social customs to local politics.

About 10 years after the Slovak immigrants first arrived, their major settlements grew to the point where the larger Slovak religious groups—the Lutherans and the Roman Catholics—could establish parishes. For the smaller groups of Greek Catholics and Calvinists, the process took longer.

Even though American and Canadian Slovaks managed to establish many parishes of all denominations throughout North America, they often had to struggle to do so. Most immigrants had lived as poor farmers and laborers in Slovakia and had no experience in establishing a parish. Still, individual laypeople, or the fraternal organizations to which they belonged, often took the lead. They raised funds, bought land, erected church buildings, and sent for priests or ministers from the old country. The laying of a church cornerstone, accompanied by elaborate ceremonies and even parades, was a major community event, even for those who did not belong to the church being built.

Slovak Lutherans, the most nationalistic of the four denominations, established the first Slovak-American parish, in Streator, Illinois, in 1884. Slovaks had begun to arrive in Illinois in the 1870s, and in 1873 they initiated Lutheran prayer services in the home of Jan Kozlej, who had come from the village of Kukova in Saris County. In 1884 Kozlej placed an advertisement for a pastor in a newspaper in Slovakia. The Reverend Cyril Droppa, from Strba in Liptov County, answered the advertisement and came to America to establish the parish of the Holy Trinity.

Many Slovak Lutheran churches arose in the United States in the years that followed, but Canada did not establish its own until 1928. Canadian Slovak Lutherans established their first church in Windsor, Ontario, that year and called it Nativity Slovak Lutheran Congregation. Subsequently other parishes appeared, but most could not afford to build actual churches until the 1940s and 1950s, when a large number of political refugees arrived.

Slovak Roman Catholic laypeople, hampered by American church politics, often had great difficulty set-

Za hrmeni... jest svetly uder zvonu
jenz mohu... cirkev vesti do sveta
ze Slovaks... jiz lamesvou poita
a Svobod... ze pvez Rozkveta

Fraternal societies organized demonstrations in support of Slovakia's fight for independence.

ting up their churches. When they raised funds, built places of worship, and recruited priests on their own, their independence annoyed the American Roman Catholic church's bishops, who were responsible for the spiritual government of Catholics within regions known as dioceses. Often, these bishops insisted that Slovaks who had built a church must sign over the church property title to the diocese. They also sought to assert their authority over priests brought over from the old country. Sometimes the Slovak Roman Catholics gave in to the bishops' demands, but occasionally they did not and instead fought the bishops in the courts, with rocks, or even with dynamite.

Slovak laypeople resisted interference by the bishops because of their experience with church authorities in Slovakia. Parishes and churches there had been built and supported largely by wealthy patrons, usually nobles. Patrons and their descendants often enjoyed special privileges in "their" churches, including control over the nomination or removal of pastors. Most of the congregation was left with little or no say in the activities of their church. Their memories of the privileges of wealthy church patrons in Slovakia inspired in Slovak immigrants a desire to retain control over their own places of worship in the New World. They also felt proud of having built their new churches with their own money and did not want to relinquish them to the American bishops. Slovak immigrants felt very strongly about these things, but their American-born children did not and gave the bishops control over the Slovak churches.

Despite these difficulties, Roman Catholic Slovaks opened their first two American parishes in December 1885—Saint Joseph's in Hazleton, Pennsylvania, and Saint Stephen's in Streator, Illinois. Many more followed in the United States, but Canadian Slovak Catholics did not establish a parish until 1906. The first was Saint Peter's Roman Catholic church in Fort William, Ontario, the largest Slovak settlement in Canada at that time. After World War I, Slovak Catholic missions sprang up in many cities in Quebec and Ontario, reflecting the arrival of larger numbers of Slovaks in these provinces. The arrival in Canada of several thousand Slovak political émigrés after World War II spurred the founding of more new Roman Catholic parishes.

Slovak Greek Catholics allied with Greek Catholics of other nationalities to form parishes in North America. The first of these was in Shenandoah, Pennsylvania, set up in 1884 by the Reverend John Volansky. The congregation included Slovaks, Rusins (Ruthenians), Hungarians, and Romanians. Because of their small numbers, Greek Catholics in America initially ignored national differences, although some groups did break away from the mixed parishes for nationalist reasons. The Greek Catholic Slovaks never established separate parishes; those with strong nationalist leanings either joined Slovak Roman Catholic parishes or gravitated toward Greek Catholic parishes with large Rusin populations. Slovak Greek Catholics did organize a few independent parishes in Canada, the first being Saints Peter and Paul in Lethbridge, Alberta, in 1921. In other parts of Canada, they generally worshiped with Slovak Roman Catholics or else in Ukrainian Greek Catholic parishes.

Calvinist Slovaks came in the smallest numbers and did not have a church until 1888. That year in Mount Carmel, Pennsylvania, the oldest Slovak Calvinist settlement in the United States, a group of Calvinists and Lutherans established a joint parish. The two groups could not agree on a preacher, however, and in 1895 the Lutherans broke away and the Calvinists joined the American Reformed Church. Because of the lack of Slovak Calvinist preachers, most Slovak Calvinist parishes established after that date called upon Czech preachers to serve them. About half of all Slovak Calvinists in America worshiped in Hungarian Calvinist parishes, giving rise to the charge among other Slovaks that Calvinists were not loyal Slovaks. Slovak Calvinists in Canada, very few in number, have not established any parishes of their own. They worship either with Slovak Lutherans or in Canadian Presbyterian churches.

Slovak parishes in the New World needed Slovak pastors and priests to serve them. At first, before the Slovaks had access to seminaries in the United States and Canada, they invited clergy to emigrate from Hungary, but the Hungarian government tried to prevent the departure of nationalist Slovak clergy, fearing the growth of New World movements to liberate Slovakia. In Slovakia and North America alike, priests and ministers served as community leaders, and those with nationalist political views often organized or participated in anti-Magyar activities.

Many of the clergy who left Hungary to serve congregations in the United States and Canada became leaders of the Slovak immigrant community. One such priest was Jozef Murgas. Born to peasant parents in the village of Tajov in Zvolen County, Slovakia, on February 17, 1864, Jozef showed great interest in both art and science in his early years of school. But because his parents could not finance his higher education, they sent him to a Roman Catholic seminary where the church paid for his education for the priesthood.

In 1889 Murgas received his ordination into the priesthood. As a Slovak nationalist, however, he did not get along with his religious superiors. Unhappy in Hungary, he responded to an advertisement in a Slovak-American newspaper for a parish priest to come to America. Murgas left Slovakia in 1896 to become the pastor of Saint Joseph's parish in Wilkes-Barre, Pennsylvania. Committed to improving the community he found there, he built a parochial school, a club, a bowling alley, and a gym very shortly after his arrival. He also edited a newspaper, *Katolik*, and helped establish a humor magazine, *Sasek*.

While continuing in his role as priest and community leader, Murgas returned to his boyhood interest in science and started experimenting with wireless telegraphy. In 1904 he took out two U.S. patents on his "tone system" of wireless telegraphy, and in 1905 he transmitted the first wireless signals, between Wilkes-Barre and Scranton, Pennsylvania, and between Wilkes-Barre and Brooklyn, New York. But a severe thunderstorm destroyed his transmitting towers, and financial difficulties forced him to suspend further experiments. Guglielmo Marconi, another inventor, later used some of Murgas's findings in his own work and claimed to have invented wireless telegraphy. In 1920 Murgas sued Marconi for patent violations. After long, drawn-out proceedings Murgas won his case.

Murgas's life as a priest, community leader, and inventor had its basis in strong national pride. He worked tirelessly for Slovak causes, and his activities during World War I showed that the Hungarian government did indeed have reason to fear Slovak nationalist clergy like him. He raised thousands of dollars for the Slovak League of America's efforts to liberate Slovakia from the Austro-Hungarian Empire. As a priest and a journalist, he inspired American Slovaks to work for the establishment of an autonomous Slovak state within a Czechoslovak federation. After the war, when the empire had collapsed and Czech and Slovak nationalists had founded a state, he returned to his native land and offered his services as a scientist to the Czechoslovak government. But because he had no formal tech-

Religious, community, and nationalist leader Jozef Murgas invented wireless telegraphy in 1904.

nical training, the government turned him down. Murgas returned to the United States in 1920 and died nine years later.

Before it lost Slovakia in 1918, the Hungarian government, in league with Magyar Roman Catholic bishops, did everything it could to keep energetic, talented, nationalist Slovak clergy like Murgas from emigrating to America, where they might cause trouble. As a result, American and Canadian Slovaks suffered from a shortage of priests and pastors, and they decided to produce their own clergy. Slovak Lutherans and Roman Catholics attended German- and Czech-American seminaries to train for the ministry, and Roman Catholics also founded a Slovak Benedictine order in the United States.

The Benedictine monks built their first abbey in Cleveland in 1922, and in 1927 they also established a boys' high school. Benedictine High became famous as one of the few Slovak Catholic high schools in America. For many years, students at Benedictine could take Slovak language classes in addition to the standard high school subjects. In 1952, the émigré Slovak historian Frantisek Hrusovsky helped establish the Slovak Institute at Benedictine High. The Slovak Institute houses the largest Slovak historical and cultural library and archives in the United States.

Slovak women called into religious service could prepare at a number of schools and convents. They could join the Slovak Sisters of Saints Cyril and Methodius or other Slovak or non-Slovak orders. The first Slovak convent in the United States was the Congregation of the Vincentian Sisters of Charity, founded in

Greek Catholics frequently named their churches for Saints Cyril and Methodius, who brought Greek Catholicism to Slovakia in the 9th century.

Braddock, Pennsylvania, in 1902. Braddock's Reverend Albert Kazinczy brought the Sisters to Pennsylvania to serve the parochial school of his parish, but they eventually relocated to Perrysville, Pennsylvania, and founded a high school for girls. Slovak immigrants helped set up many other orders in North America as well.

Slovaks in the United States and Canada wasted no time creating a large quantity and variety of religious institutions to fulfill their spiritual needs. In 1930 the number of New World Slovak parishes peaked. American Slovaks worshiped in 241 Roman Catholic, 48 Lutheran, and 9 Calvinist parishes of their own, while Greek Catholics attended 155 non-Slovak churches. Although the establishment of so many Slovak parishes in so short a period testifies to the religious commitment of the people, it also highlights the deep divisions within the community.

Slovaks of all sects lived together in the same communities, but each sect's priests and pastors feared "mixed marriages" and warned against social contact with Slovaks of different denominations. Within settlements, therefore, each religious group formed a distinct community with its own churches and fraternal organizations. The Slovak-American and Canadian-Slovak communities remain divided by denomination today, but throughout their history all Slovaks have been united by their devout adherence to the Judeo-Christian tradition.

Slovaks arriving from Europe, proud of their religious and cultural heritage, set up fraternal benefit societies and church parishes to help preserve their national identity. They kept the holidays as they always had and established schools to teach their American-born children and grandchildren Slovak language and traditions. In their boardinghouses, saloons, and lodges, Slovak immigrants hoped to reproduce some of the feelings of village life; and in their diet, dress, and music they strove to keep the old customs alive. ❧

Many Slovak children found their first jobs in the coal mines, picking slate out of the coal through a "breaker," or grate, under their feet.

ORDINARY DAYS AND HOLIDAYS

Churches and fraternal benefit societies played a central role in the life of Slovak immigrants, providing a sense of community and perpetuating Slovak ethnicity in the New World. Most of the immigrants hoped to recreate their ancestral culture in order to feel at home in North America and also to give their children a sense of their heritage. Toward these ends, they established parochial schools to educate their children in the Slovak language and according to Slovak traditions and morality. Teaching children to follow the old ways and beliefs was as important in the Slovak parochial schools as teaching them to read and write.

Slovak Parochial Schools in the New World

Mindful of their experiences in Europe, Slovak immigrants brought a fear of and contempt for public schools with them to North America. Before the fall of the Austro-Hungarian Empire, the Hungarian government had sought to assimilate Slovaks into Hungarian culture. They declared Magyar the official language, took over the Slovak parochial schools, and taught Slovak children to read and write in Magyar rather than Slovak. Slovak immigrant parents thus preferred not to send their children to American public schools for fear

Immigrants preserved many of their customs, including the playing of native folk songs, in the New World.

that they would not have control over what their children learned.

Prompted by this concern, many Roman Catholic parishes and some Lutheran parishes opened parochial schools soon after they built their churches. The Roman Catholics, however, had some difficulty establishing their schools because of a shortage of Slovak nuns qualified to serve as teaching sisters. Although the Irish, Polish, and other Catholic parochial schools in America easily found staff among nuns from the old country or from convents they had started in America, the Slovak schools could not. Until 1909, Slovaks had no New World convents of their own. In addition, the Hungarian government and church required absolute loyalty from the sisters teaching there, so Slovaks in North America did not have access to nuns from Slovakia.

To solve the problem, the Reverend Matus Jankola of Hazleton, Pennsylvania, began raising funds in 1899 to found an order of Slovak teaching nuns in the United States. But the Congregation of the Sisters of Saints Cyril and Methodius, established in Danville, Pennsylvania, in 1909, never attracted enough members to staff all the Slovak parochial schools in the United States. By 1930 the 241 Slovak-American Catholic parishes operated 127 schools, but only one third of these employed Slovak teaching sisters. This shortage meant that most Slovak-American children who enrolled in parochial schools were not taught in Slovak. The schools could not therefore fulfill two of their primary functions—teaching the Slovak language and reinforcing Slovak culture—and the immigrants' children eagerly adopted the English language, which eased their assimilation into mainstream American culture.

Slovak Lutherans established parochial Saturday or summer schools where children learned the Slovak language and the tenets of Lutheranism while receiving their academic education in American public schools. Slovak Greek Catholic children usually attended Greek Catholic or Roman Catholic parochial schools or went to public school. But only those who found a Slovak parochial school were taught in the Slovak language. Slovak Calvinists, too small in number to establish their own schools, sent their children to the local public schools.

Canadian Slovaks had virtually no opportunity to send their children to Slovak schools to learn their native language. In Fort William, Ontario, Roman Catholic Slovaks could attend Saint Peter's parochial school, but its staff employed no Slovak teaching sisters. The children received their lessons in English and had only occasional access to Slovak language courses taught by laypeople. Most Slovak children in Canada studied at parochial or public schools staffed by English-speaking teachers.

The children of Slovak immigrants generally started school at age six. In Catholic parochial schools, the day started with mass at 8:00 A.M., during which the children had to kneel facing the altar. The typical morning might include reading, writing, and arithmetic classes, followed by a half-hour recess at 10:00 A.M. and more of the three Rs. After a noontime lunch at home, the students returned to study subjects such as geography, civics (social studies), and art. Usually on Friday afternoons, the nuns taught Slovak language, history, and songs.

Everyday Life

When school was out, children attended to chores such as herding the family geese and picking coal from train cars for the stove at home. On Sundays, the children had plenty of duties as well, such as picking wild berries or mushrooms in the woods or collecting wood for fuel. They also had time for play and enjoyed swimming, games of tag and hide and seek, and other activities.

Unfortunately, most immigrant families were very poor, so many children, when they finished seventh or eighth grade, went to work to supplement the family income. The coal mines and silk mills illegally hired children as young as 9 years old and paid them as little as 3 cents an hour to work 10-hour days. Because even their small income made a difference at home, only 20 percent of the early immigrants' children graduated from high school.

The first Slovak children born in North America grew up surrounded by the traditions of Slovakia. The food they ate, the music they listened to, and the way they celebrated holidays all bore the imprint of the Old World. Their parents, the nuns at school, and the parish priests taught them Slovak ways, but the children saw the New World around them and wanted to discover it. Born American, most of them hoped to grow up as thoroughly American as the children of their parents' bosses. Thus, while the first generation hoped to keep the Slovak heritage alive, the process of assimilation began in earnest with those immigrants' children who wanted to leave their "Hunky" past.

Even before their American children were born, however, the Slovak immigrants themselves had already taken a few steps toward assimilation, most notably in the way they dressed. In Slovakia they had worn two kinds of clothes: On most days, Slovak laborers wore simple, homemade linen clothing, usually white, in seasonal weights, and for holidays and special occasions, men and women both wore elaborately embroidered folk dress. The style of embroidery varied from village to village by region and according to the wearer's station in life; eastern Slovakia favored geometric decoration, whereas central and western Slovakia more often used realistic designs with floral motifs.

Slovaks arriving in the United States and Canada quickly adopted turn-of-the-century fashions. Men wore black suits for formal occasions and jeans or overalls for their work in the mines and mills; women retained their traditional dress for a few years but soon bowed to mainstream fashion. They bought everyday clothes in American stores and wore white dresses on Sundays, unpacking their traditional costumes only for weddings, dances, and other special occasions.

The Slovak immigrants changed their diets only slightly when they moved to the New World. In Slo-

Parochial schools instilled Slovak-American children with the religious values of their parents.

vakia they had typically eaten a rather simple diet of potatoes, cheese, milk, and thick vegetable soups laced with vinegar or sour cream. Sometimes they supplemented this fare with fruit in the summer and fall or sauerkraut, sausage, and other preserved foods in the winter. On Sundays they often consumed chicken soup and pastry, and on special occasions they might have duck, pork, or goose. Slovaks liberally spiced most of their food with paprika, a taste they shared with Hungarians.

In the New World the Slovak diet broadened to include more meat, which was much cheaper here than in Slovakia. Especially after they had their first taste of steak in the saloons, the immigrants quickly adopted the custom of eating meat whenever they could afford it. But the rest of their diet remained almost unchanged for many years after they had arrived in North America. Not until the immigrants' children and grandchildren tired of preparing time-consuming traditional recipes did Slovak Americans and Canadian Slovaks make major changes in their diet. Then they embraced American dishes such as meat loaf, macaroni and cheese, and hamburgers.

Slovak tastes in music also changed over time. In their homeland the Slovaks had favored folk melodies, waltzes, czardas, and polkas, which they played themselves or heard performed by roving Gypsy bands. The immigrants brought their music with them and continued to sing the same folk songs in the saloons and play the same melodies at dances, weddings, and other celebrations. Slovak, Hungarian, Polish, and Czech polka bands sprang up in the New World to perform the traditional music, which Slovak Americans and Canadians continued to enjoy for many years. Those born in North America, however, preferred to listen and dance to the popular current tunes they heard on the radio and played on jukeboxes and phonographs.

In addition to American music, Slovaks discovered American and Canadian sports. Perhaps because of their fathers' heavy drinking and their mothers' warnings about alcohol, the immigrants' children took to sports rather than to drinking as a way to relax. Many fraternal benefit societies formed baseball, football, gymnastics, and other teams. They competed in tournaments against other Slovak fraternals or against teams set up by other ethnic groups. Getting their starts in schoolyards and abandoned lots, many Americans and Canadians of Slovak extraction have in fact excelled at professional sports.

In glass factories, child laborers like this seated "mold boy" worked four and a half hours at a stretch before earning a half-hour break.

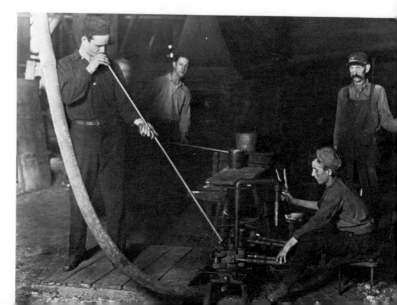

On special occasions, Slovak immigrants wore their native costumes and hired polka bands to play traditional music.

The story of Charles (Chuck) Bednarik, for example, is not only that of a great athlete, but also that of a second-generation Slovak American who successfully assimilated into American culture. He was born in Bethlehem, Pennsylvania, on May 1, 1925, to parents who had immigrated to America just after World War I. He graduated from Saints Cyril and Methodius Slovak parochial school in 1939 and, against his mother's wishes, chose to attend public high schools so he could take advantage of the sports programs they offered.

Since childhood, Chuck had played football with his friends in South Bethlehem. He loved the game and was determined to become a professional. His size and talent earned him a place on the teams of the two high schools he attended—teams that won several championships with his help. When he graduated from high school in 1943, he temporarily left the gridiron because the air force drafted him to serve in World War II. He flew 30 combat missions in a heavy bomber and was promoted to sergeant before he returned to Pennsylvania in 1945.

Bednarik enrolled at the University of Pennsylvania and soon helped turn its football team into a winner. Playing both center and middle linebacker, Bednarik was named to the All-American team in 1948. After completing his studies, he signed with the Philadelphia Eagles of the National Football League. Playing both offense and defense for the Eagles, he achieved the distinction of All-Pro. Bednarik's talent contributed to some of the best season records the Eagles had ever had. In their 1960 championship season he stayed on the field for the full 60 minutes of each game. "The last

"The last of the sixty-minute men," Chuck Bednarik (number 60), played both offense and defense for the Philadelphia Eagles from 1949 to 1960.

of the 60-minute men" retired in 1961 and was one of the first players elected to the football Hall of Fame.

Several Slovak Canadians have played professional hockey, most notably Stanley Mikita. Born May 20, 1940, in Sokolce, Liptov County, Slovakia, Mikita came to Canada with his family after World War II. He grew up in Saint Catharines, Ontario, where he played hockey on the streets and in ice rinks. He attracted professional attention as the star of his high-school team and in 1958 joined the Chicago Blackhawks.

Mikita enjoyed a spectacular career with the Blackhawks. As the team's center, he won the Art Ross Trophy (for the most points scored by any player in the league) every year from 1964 through 1968, except 1966. In 1967 and 1968 he received both the Hart Trophy, which recognizes the league's most valuable player, and the Lady Byng Trophy for sportsmanship. The author of two books, *I Play to Win* (1969) and *Inside Hockey* (1971), Stan Mikita retired in the early 1970s and was elected to the hockey Hall of Fame.

The younger generation of Slovaks in the United States and Canada found sports an area in which they could achieve assimilation more easily than in other areas. They had trouble fitting into the workplace because their American and Irish bosses still considered them "Hunkies," even though they spoke without foreign accents and understood American ways. On the social plane as well, the immigrants' children found assimilation somewhat difficult. They remained outside mainstream society because, for the most part, they still lived in ethnic neighborhoods and kept the old traditions.

Intermarriage with other ethnic groups is a common means of assimilating, but for years Slovaks largely kept to themselves. The immigrants had almost never married non-Slovaks, and about two-thirds of the members of the second generation also married other Slovaks. Even the one-third that married non-Slovaks stayed close to their heritage: They usually married members of culturally similar ethnic groups such as Czechs, Hungarians, Poles, and Ukrainians. Assimilation through intermarriage became acceptable only with later generations; fewer than half of the immigrants' grandchildren and great-grandchildren married others of Slovak descent, and those who married non-Slovaks began to marry a greater proportion of people of northern and western European heritage.

Stan Mikita immigrated to Canada as a child and later rose to fame as the center for the Chicago Blackhawks. He is shown here scoring his 500th goal.

Celebrations and Holidays

When they did marry, Slovak immigrants and their children liked to celebrate in the traditional Slovak way, although they gradually adapted their customs to the realities of life in North America. Couples wishing to marry had to obtain the permission of their parents, which they did in an elaborate ceremony. In the old country, the parents of the bride and groom arranged a dowry, but immigrants to North America dropped the practice. In preparation for the wedding, the bride's parents hired musicians and made arrangements to provide a lavish spread of food and drink.

On their wedding day, the bride and groom formally asked their parents for forgiveness and blessing, then rode to church in a decorated coach or wagon. They solemnized their vows in a ceremony there, and afterward the wedding party marched together to a fraternal lodge hall or other gathering place for the celebration. A master of ceremonies entertained the revelers with

jokes and stories as everyone ate and drank. The drinking continued as the dancing started. Gypsy bands or polka bands performed traditional waltzes, polkas, and wild czardas, and the dancing went on until dawn.

At midnight the groom was banished from the dance floor, and the bride danced a farewell dance with her family. Her mother gave her a "kerchief of womanhood," which married women in Slovakia traditionally wore whenever they went out of doors. The kerchief—referred to as a babushka—indicated to the world that the woman who wore it was married and unavailable for courting. After receiving the kerchief, the bride danced with anyone who paid a small fee, thereby collecting a stake for her future. The money she collected replaced the dowry paid by brides' parents in Slovakia. After the wedding dance ended, the bride joined the groom in their new home, usually a room in the groom's father's house. Young married couples typically lived with their families until they could afford to move into homes of their own.

Slovaks enjoyed large wedding celebrations, which provided some relief from the grim struggle of daily existence.

Family members and fellow fraternalists paid their respects to the deceased at funerals that sometimes cost the family's entire savings.

In communities scattered across the United States and Canada, the first two generations of Slovaks carried on the tradition of these highly formal weddings, although few celebrations went on for the two days to two weeks that had been common in Slovakia. Even today, some of the customs appear at the weddings of those descended from Slovak immigrants. Wedding entertainers still play some of the old dances, mixed in with more contemporary music, and mothers still bestow the "kerchief of womanhood" upon their daughters, although American-born women have refused to wear it. As assimilation runs its course, however, fewer and fewer Slovaks practice the old wedding customs.

When Slovaks started families in the New World, they continued their tradition of christening newborn children. The christening ceremony served to bring children into both the church and the community. It included the naming of godparents, who would take responsibility for the child's welfare if the parents died. By linking the families of the parents and the godparents, this tradition strengthened the Slovak community.

In addition to a ceremony, each christening included the chanting of ancient pagan incantations to ward off evil spirits. Slovaks feared that forces such as the "evil eye," if they were not banished immediately, might curse their children. Parents invited practically the entire town to take part in the festivities that followed the christening. Slovak immigrants and their children preserved the custom of large, elaborate christenings, but their descendants no longer hold such extravagant celebrations.

Just as christenings provided the Slovak community an opportunity to greet new members, funerals gave it occasion to mark appropriately the passing of those who had died. Slovak families laid out the body of the deceased for a few days so that friends and colleagues could take their leave of the loved one. During this time, the family provided food and drink to the mourners—usually all the Slovaks in town—who came to pay their respects. The immigrants' children dropped this tradition when some of them became professional funeral directors, and the younger generations preferred to follow the American practice of holding their wakes in funeral homes.

After the wake, the Slovaks held a complicated church ceremony and burial, with a long and colorful funeral procession. Dressed in full lodge regalia, all fraternal society members attended the funerals of those belonging to their lodge. By paying death benefits to their members' survivors and attending their members' funerals, the fraternals fulfilled one of their more important functions. The immigrants' children carried on this tradition, but third-generation Slovaks have modified it. Typically, only one or two lodge officers now attend a member's funeral, and they no longer wear their uniforms to the ceremony.

The Slovaks' respect for life showed up not only in their solemn observance of death but also in their joyous Easter festivals. Easter combined the Christian celebration of the resurrection of Christ with ancient Slovak rites marking the earth's springtime renewal. Slovak Catholics prepared for this major feast day by going to confession and communion and preparing special Easter baskets. On Holy Saturday, the parish priest blessed these baskets, which contained hand-painted

Easter eggs and other treats symbolic of the rebirth of nature.

On Easter day the immigrants went to church and later ate the contents of their Easter baskets. The next day Slovak men doused their wives or girlfriends with water in a fertility rite. The women performed the same ritual on Easter Tuesday, pouring pots or cups of water over their husbands or boyfriends. This custom survived for two generations, but it is now rapidly disappearing. Today the Slovak community celebrates Easter in much the same way that other Americans and Canadians do.

In both the New World and the Old, Slovaks held distinctive Christmas celebrations. The Slovak Christmas season began on December 6, when Catholics kept the tradition of a visit from Saint Nicholas. According to this custom, Saint Nicholas visited children's homes, accompanied by an angel and devil, to question children and their parents about the children's behavior. The angel gave good children gifts from Saint Nicholas's large sack, and the devil gave bad children a spanking.

In the two weeks following Saint Nicholas's visit, the Slovaks baked Christmas pastries. The aroma of baking poppy-seed rolls, nut pastries, and gingerbread

Slovak Americans still prepare Easter pastries according to recipes brought from the Old World by immigrants.

cookies filled their kitchens while young women told each other's fortunes. To determine where the men they would marry might come from, they threw shoes over their shoulders. Another technique they used was to melt some lead, pour it into a cup of water, hold the solidified form up to the light of a candle, and read the future in the shadow it cast.

After weeks of preparation, Christmas Eve, the most important day of the winter, arrived. Christian Slovaks fasted all day, but as soon as a child of the family sighted the first evening star, a sumptuous Christmas Eve meal began. A father or grandfather offered an elaborate prayer of thanksgiving, and then a mother distributed communion wafers covered with honey. Family members cut apples across the center to see how their luck would run in the new year. If a core made the shape of a star, then good luck would come in the new year; if not, then bad luck would. The young women of the family cracked walnuts to read their fortunes. If the young woman found healthy meat in the nuts, she would have good luck in finding a husband.

An enormous meal followed the fortune-telling. Hot mulled wine accompanied sauerkraut soup or soup made from sauerkraut brine; then came fried fish or *klobasa* sausage; *macanka* (mushroom sauce); bean and potato salads; and *pupaky*, *opekance*, or *bobalky* (pieces

The immigrants' Christmas festivities quickly acquired a New World accent.

of bread covered with crushed poppy-seed sauce or hot butter and cottage cheese). After the main course, the family ate half a dozen different kinds of poppy-seed and nut pastries as well as fruit and nuts. Then, if they kept livestock, they gathered up the leftovers and gave them to the animals.

Tradition held that the infant Jesus visited each Slovak household on Christmas Eve and left presents. On Christmas Eve, families sang carols when they finished their dinner and then opened their presents, which lay under an evergreen tree decorated with candles, fruit, cookies, candies, sparklers, and tinsel. At midnight, Slovak Catholics attended mass. Families spent Christmas day at home together, enjoying their presents and the holiday.

Between December 26 (Saint Stephen's Day) and January 6 (the Feast of the Epiphany), children dressed up as shepherds (*jaslickari*) or the three Magi (*bethlehemci*) and went from house to house each evening. They sang Christmas carols in return for gifts of food for themselves and money for the church. During this time, neighbors visited to wish one another a merry Christmas. When visiting, the men of the family made sure to enter their neighbors' households before the women, because they believed a household would have bad luck in the new year if a woman entered it ahead of a man.

Slovak immigrants and their children kept up these Christmas traditions for many years, but Slovak Americans and Canadians today have given up most of them in favor of the New World's Santa Claus. In almost every aspect of their lives, in fact, the grandchildren and great-grandchildren of the Slovak immigrants prefer to follow the customs of North America. Only the aging immigrants and second-generation Slovaks keep the old ways, and their descendants have an increasingly dim notion of their Slovak heritage. Although this seems unfortunate to some of the older generation, it demonstrates how successfully people of Slovak descent have assimilated into American and Canadian culture.

Barred from the United States by restrictive quotas, Slovaks immigrated to Canada after World War I, often farming in the western provinces.

CULTURAL VITALITY

After World War I, in 1924, Slovak immigration to the United States virtually halted because the United States Congress had instituted a discriminatory immigration quota system. The system set limits on the number of people from each country who could enter the United States each year, favoring northern and western Europeans and discriminating against southern and eastern Europeans such as the Slovaks.

Faced with the difficulty of entering the United States, Slovaks headed for Canada in increasing numbers. Relatively unpopulated, Canada welcomed immigrants, particularly if they wanted to farm. In fact, Canadian consular officials in Slovakia during the 1920's inspected the hands of prospective immigrants for calluses, telltale signs of their ability to do the hard work necessary to start a farm in the Canadian West.

Canadian authorities wanted the immigrants to settle the West and sent all Slovaks to Winnipeg, Manitoba, known as the gateway to Canada's prairie provinces. Once in Winnipeg, the immigrants had to fend for themselves. But although they tried to make a go of it, most could not find enough work to make life in the Canadian West worth their while. Farmhands

The large population of Slovak Greek Catholics in Canada has its own bishop, the Reverend Michael Rusnak, consecrated in 1965.

worked only in the spring and summer months; in the fall and winter they could find work cutting timber, but the harshness of the Canadian winter made this job almost unbearable. Unhappy with conditions in the West, most of the Slovaks who came to Canada in the 1920s and 1930s eventually found their way to Montreal, Quebec, or Toronto, Ontario. There they found steady work and established large and thriving settlements.

During World War II, immigration from Europe stopped temporarily, but after the war, Canada continued to attract Slovak immigrants. Whereas the United States set strict rules regarding which of the millions of people displaced by the war could gain entry to the country, Canada opened its borders to all. As a result, most political refugees from Slovakia (which had become part of Soviet-dominated Czechoslovakia) went to Canada.

The refugees arriving in Canada included many Greek Catholic laypeople and priests, because the communist government of Czechoslovakia (which took over in 1948) abolished the Greek Catholic church in 1950. These émigré priests and parishioners established six new parishes and two missions in Canada within a decade of their arrival. Slovak Greek Catholics in Canada established such a vital community (though by no means the largest Greek Catholic colony) that in 1980 they gained their own bishop, the only Slovak Greek Catholic bishop in the world.

Slovak immigrants to Canada after World War II also included members of Slovakia's intelligentsia. Having fled their homeland to escape political persecution, they brought with them pride in their ethnic heritage and concern for the fate of Slovaks in Czechoslovakia. Because the intellectuals revived Slovak nationalism and the use of the Slovak language, their arrival had a rejuvenating effect on the Canadian Slovak community. Thanks in large part to their presence, the Canadian Slovak community still retains much of its ethnic identity today.

New World Intellectuals and Artists

Because most Slovak intellectuals chose to stay in Hungary in order to fight the Magyar government's efforts at assimilating the Slovak people, very few immigrated to North America before World War I. Those who did leave were often priests who went to the New World to minister to the growing number of Slovaks living there. Others, such as nationalist newspaper editors and schoolteachers, had been driven out for political reasons by the government.

In the New World, the few Slovak intellectuals produced many newspapers, almanacs, books, pamphlets, and plays, many with a nationalist flavor. Like the Slovak fraternal benefit societies, the intellectuals shared a concern for Slovak ethnicity and often found vehicles for their opinions in the publications produced by those organizations. Whether published by fraternal societies or independent journalists, Slovak newspapers in both the United States and Canada met the immigrants' vital need for information. One of the first Slovak Americans to get into the newspaper business was Peter Rovnianek, the founder of the National Slovak Society (see Chapter 3). In 1888, while still in seminary, he had begun to write nationalist articles for *Amerikanszko-Szlovenszke Novini*, the first Slovak newspaper in America. A year later, he moved to Pittsburgh, Pennsylvania, where the paper was published, and took over its editorship. Under Rovnianek's guidance, the paper became the leading Slovak nationalist weekly in North America. In addition, his work on the paper demonstrates the central place of language in nationalist movements. Following the rules of literary Slovak, he carefully standardized the spelling and grammar used in the paper and corrected the newspaper's name to *Amerikansko-Slovenske Noviny*.

Rovnianek used his unique editorial skills to awaken the spirit of Slovak nationalism among his readers. He attacked the Hungarian government outright in his articles and praised the czar's Russian Empire. His hope

that the Russians would liberate Slovakia from Hungary, expressed in pro-Russian editorials, led the Russian government to name him Russian vice-consul in Pittsburgh in 1907.

Rovnianek also tried his hand at business, with less success. In the early 1890s he established the P.V. Rovnianek Company, which sold steamship tickets to Slovaks, and he became quite wealthy. Thousands of American Slovaks and Slovak immigrants entrusted money to him to pay the way to America for themselves or their relatives. Unfortunately for them, Rovnianek invested these funds unwisely. In 1911 his firm went bankrupt, and Rovnianek fled to the American West to escape the ire of his creditors and depositors. He tried to recover some of his losses by prospecting for gold, but he died in poverty in California on November 16, 1933.

Rovnianek's longtime rival, Stefan Furdek, also knew the importance of maintaining a Slovak press and literature. When Furdek established the First Catholic Slovak Union, one of its main functions was to publish the Slovak Catholic weekly *Jednota*. Today, the paper has the largest circulation of any Slovak newspaper in the Western world. For 20 years Furdek served as *Jednota's* editor. The hundreds of articles he published in its pages (as well as in the almanac of the same name) exhorted Slovaks to have pride in their heritage. Furdek also wrote many books of practical advice for immigrants on how to live in America, and he composed poems and songs about the beauty of his native land.

Furdek's work in the Slovak community, journalistic and otherwise, made him one of the most beloved Slovak leaders of his time, earning him the name "father of American Slovaks." In 1908 the bishop of Cleveland named Furdek vicar-general of East European nationalities in the Cleveland diocese. His concern for all Eastern European immigrants inspired a rare sense of unity among the various subgroups in his diocese. When Furdek died on January 18, 1915, he was mourned by all Slovaks.

Many nationalist Slovak intellectuals followed Rovnianek and Furdek into the journalistic arena in the New World. Since 1885 American and Canadian Slovaks have established over 220 daily, weekly, and monthly periodicals. Supported by large organizations, the fraternal newspapers have generally lasted longest, but many others have gone out of business as Slovak readership has dwindled. The periodicals have expressed a range of political and religious views, but all have served a valuable function by reporting news of interest to all Slovaks and by publishing, at least initially or in part, in the Slovak language.

Although newspapers and almanacs have provided a medium for Slovak expression and have offered some insight into the Slovak experience in North America, they scarcely qualify as literature. A small group of Slovak intellectuals, disturbed that the world at large had not recognized Slovak contributions to the arts, came to the United States and Canada after World War II hoping to stimulate some interest in Slovak art and literature.

A number of poets and short-story writers published in American and Canadian Slovak newspapers and almanacs, and a group of these writers founded the Slovak literary review *Most* (published since 1954). Because they wrote exclusively in Slovak, however, none of these writers managed to establish a reputation outside the Slovak community.

Even among the Slovak population, only a handful of people read these writers. For the most part, working-class Slovaks lacked the time, money, and inclination to patronize the arts. A few American- and Canadian-born Slovaks writing in English have, however, achieved critical and popular success, and two Slovak-American painters have received some attention from the Czechoslovak government and from North American critics.

The pressroom at Jednota, *the newspaper founded by Reverend Stefan Furdek in Middletown, Pennsylvania.*

Among Slovak-American writers, Thomas Bell and Paul Wilkes have gained the greatest recognition. Bell (originally Belejcak) was born on March 7, 1903, in Braddock, Pennsylvania. His father, Michael Belejcak,

had immigrated from Saris County in Slovakia, and his mother, Maria Kracun Belejcak, was the daughter of Slovak immigrants. Both of Bell's parents died of tuberculosis; his father when Bell was 11, and his mother when he was 16. Bell read voraciously as a boy; a thrilling moment of his childhood came when he received a library card from the local library. But because of his father's death, he had to drop out of school at age 14 to work. He found his first job in a glass works and later went on to a job in a steel mill. During his teenage years, Bell studied on his own and took up writing, often coming home from 12-hour factory shifts to sit at his typewriter until 4 o'clock in the morning. At the same time, he found the energy to write a column for the Braddock *News Herald*.

At the age of 19, Bell left his hometown and for the next few years made his living on ocean freighters. He then settled in New York City, where he worked at odd jobs. By 1930 he had earned enough money to send for his brother and one of his two sisters in Braddock (the other had married). He took care of them until he met and married Marie Benedetti in 1932. His wife then supported him while he launched his writing career. During the early 1930s, Bell published two commercially unsuccessful novels, but his luck turned when he published *All Brides Are Beautiful* in 1936. Based on his happy marriage, the book tells the story of one couple's life in the Bronx during the Great Depression. The novel received excellent reviews, went into several printings, and came out as a Hollywood film, *From This Day Forward*, in 1946.

In 1941 Bell published his masterpiece, *Out of This Furnace*. The novel traces the experiences of a Slovak-American family in Braddock, Pennsylvania, beginning with the arrival of a young man from Slovakia in 1880 and concluding with his grandson's involvement in the formation of a steelworkers' labor union in 1937. *Out of This Furnace* portrays, dramatically and in great detail, the hardships endured by Slovak immigrants and

Journalism enabled nationalist Slovak Americans to voice their opinions.

In 1946 Joan Fontaine starred in From This Day Forward, *the film adaptation of Thomas Bell's novel* All Brides Are Beautiful.

their descendants in the steel towns of Pennsylvania. Bell addressed a similar theme in *There Comes a Time* (1946), an account of a bank employee who tries to organize his co-workers into a union.

Shortly thereafter, when Bell developed writer's block, he moved to California with his wife and opened a stationery store. A few years later he contracted cancer, and in the last two years of his life he penned the remarkable *In the Midst of Life*, a memoir published posthumously in 1961.

While Thomas Bell approached the end of his life, another Slovak American, Paul Wilkes (originally Vilk), was preparing to become a writer. Born of Slovak-American parents in Cleveland, Ohio, on September 12, 1938, he received a B.A. in journalism from Marquette University in 1960. He went on to earn an M.A. from the Columbia University School of Journalism in 1967. Wilkes put his education to work writing for the *Boulder Daily Camera* and the *Baltimore Sun*, as well as for a number of national magazines.

In 1973 Wilkes published his first novel, *Fitzgo, the Wild Dog of Central Park*, and in 1974, *These Priests Stay*. That same year, he received awards from the Society of Midland Writers and the Friends of American Writers. He wrote *Trying Out the Dream* in 1975, and in 1977 Marquette University bestowed upon him its Byline Award. His book *Six American Families* (1978), based on a PBS television series, won the du Pont-Columbia Award for documentary excellence in 1978, the same year that Columbia University gave him its Distinguished Alumni Award. In 1984 Wilkes published *Merton by Those Who Knew Him Best*, which aired as a PBS series the same year. He continues to write today and has chosen the tentative title *In Due Season* for his next book, a nonfiction account of Slovak immigration to the United States.

In the field of fine art, two Slovak Americans, Kolomon Sokol and Alvena Seckar, have achieved recognition. Kolomon Sokol was born on December 12, 1902, in Liptov County in Slovakia. Between 1920 and 1933, after completing his high school education, he studied art under various masters in the Slovak cities of Kosice and Bratislava and also went to Prague and Paris. When he returned to Slovakia from Paris, he quickly gained a reputation as one of the best graphic artists in the country.

Not content with his success in Slovakia, Sokol left for Mexico City in 1936. There, he found a position as a professor of graphic arts at Mexican National University. Soon, however, the country's widespread poverty and the Mexican government's failure to help its suffering citizens caused Sokol to emigrate again to the

Novelist, journalist, and television writer Paul Wilkes has received many awards.

United States. A Baltimore, Maryland, gallery held a major 1942 show of the paintings Sokol had done in Mexico; the realist paintings portrayed the suffering of the Mexican people.

While in the United States, Sokol joined the expatriate Slovaks' World War II movement to liberate Czechoslovakia from the Nazis, and after the war he returned to his homeland a hero. He taught graphic arts at the Comenius University of Bratislava until the communists seized control of the government in 1948. When he left for the United States, settling in Bryn Mawr, Pennsylvania, the communist government of Czechoslovakia declared Sokol's art "full of bourgeois formalism and decadence" and officially declared him a nonperson.

In 1963 Alexander Dubcek, the liberal secretary of the Slovak Communist party, reinstated Sokol into the party's good graces. Sokol's canvases hung again in the Slovak National Gallery, and since then Sokol has had many shows in Slovakia. The Czechoslovak government has called on him to return home, but he prefers to live in Bryn Mawr, secluded and relatively obscure.

Alvena V. Seckar has also met with success as an artist. Born on March 1, 1916, to Slovak parents in McMechen, West Virginia, Alvena saw her alcoholic father for the last time in 1924, when her mother Susan walked out on him, taking Alvena with her. They moved to a succession of towns, finally settling in Allentown, Pennsylvania, where Mrs. Seckar opened a small restaurant and grocery store.

A sixth-grade schoolteacher recognized Alvena's talent for drawing and painting and persuaded wealthy patrons to send her to art classes on Saturdays and in the summer. In 1935 Seckar won a scholarship to the University of Pennsylvania. She studied there for three years but was asked to leave because of her radical politics. She then enrolled at New York University, receiving a B.A. in fine arts in 1939 and a scholarship to attend the School of Art and Archeology at NYU. As part of her studies, Seckar traveled all over the world.

At the age of 71, Alvena Seckar continues to paint despite crippling multiple sclerosis.

She had her first solo show in 1944 at a gallery in New York City and her second in 1946 at the Pittsburgh Art and Crafts Center. Both exhibits featured Seckar's bleak West Virginia landscapes. According to the *Pittsburgh Courier*, her starkly realistic paintings depicted the "grim side of mine life."

In 1949 Seckar received her M.A. from NYU. In the 1950s she wrote a series of children's books about the life of Slovak immigrants in West Virginia. One of these, *Zuska of the Burning Hills*, won a place on the *New York Times* list of the 100 best books published for children in 1952. Her work has recently attracted the attention of the Czechoslovak government, which arranged a Seckar exhibit at the Bratislava City Museum in 1984. Now afflicted with multiple sclerosis, Seckar can paint only with her left hand. *Newsweek* magazine honored her in 1986 as one of America's "unsung heroes" for her courage in the face of adversity.

Seckar's life spans the period during which Slovaks have come into their own as Americans and Canadians, and her story has ingredients in common with more typical second- and third-generation Slovaks in North America. From her birth in a mining town to her steeltown childhood, and from her assimilation into mainstream American culture to her continued contact with her ancestral homeland, Seckar shares the experiences of hundreds of thousands of Slovak Americans and Canadian Slovaks in the 20th century. ∾

Americans and Canadians of Slovak descent have thoroughly assimilated, but they still enjoy festivals celebrating their ethnic heritage.

THE SLOVAK COMMUNITY TODAY

Although some Slovak Americans and Canadian Slovaks— immigrant intellectuals and also the descendants of immigrant laborers—have made lasting contributions to art and literature, the vast majority have led lives circumscribed by the necessity of earning a living in heavy industry. Now, however, the descendants of Slovak immigrants pursue university education in increasing numbers, usually with the goal of entering the professions. Education in American and Canadian institutions has allowed people of Slovak ancestry to assimilate completely and make their "Hunky" roots a distant memory.

Among the grandchildren and great-grandchildren of the Slovak immigrants, almost none can speak the Slovak language. Many have changed their names to make them sound less foreign, and many others have married people from other ethnic groups, taken their names, and adopted some of their ways. The younger generations have developed new tastes in food, music, and entertainment and have accepted the values of the New World.

Political refugees have revived the nationalist feelings of Slovak Canadians, who periodically protest Soviet domination of Czechoslovakia. Here, Press Attaché Vladimar Makhotis hears shouts of angry protest as he leaves the Soviet Embassy in Ottawa.

The evolution of the Slovak community's newspapers demonstrates the extent to which assimilation has progressed. The earliest newspapers were published exclusively in the Slovak language. Later, they included special Slovak-language supplements for children, but after World War II these supplements appeared in English, evidence that fewer young Slovak Americans understood Slovak. As the first and second generation of readers aged and died, many Slovak publications lost their readership and had to close down.

Today Slovak papers print their front sections in English and their back sections in Slovak—and the back sections shrink each year. Most Americans and Canadians of Slovak descent now get their news from the same papers read by everyone else. Older Slovaks mourn the loss of their language in the New World, but their children's and grandchildren's ability to speak and read English as their native tongue has given these younger Slovaks distinct economic and social advantages in North America.

The practice of changing their names to make them sound more American has also helped. The Slovak language, and most Slovak names, use diacritical marks (special accent marks) to show which of many possible pronunciations to use for each vowel. Because English speakers found diacritical marks confusing, immigrants to the New World stopped using them in their names. They also changed the form of their surnames. Slovak surnames have different endings for men and women; for instance, if male members of a family have the surname *Ivanco*, female members use *Ivancova*. But in America and Canada, both male and female members of their family adopt the single name *Ivanco*.

The difficulty most Americans and Canadians had understanding Slovak pronunciation led most people with Slovak names to make some kind of adaptation. Some Ivancos might choose to spell their name as they pronounce it, *Evancho*. Others might retain the original spelling but pronounce the name *Ivanko*, as most English speakers do. New World-born descendants of Slovaks also choose English-sounding first names for their children instead of the saints' names traditionally used in Slovakia. These changes have all served as a means to assimilate and as a sign of assimilation.

Slovak families in North America have also altered their family life-style. Slovak immigrants and their children often lived in extended families, with children, parents, grandparents, cousins, aunts, uncles, and in-laws all under the same roof, and the first Slovaks in the New World extended their families even further than they had in Slovakia, taking boarders into their homes and treating them as members of the family. The grandchildren of the immigrants, however, adopted the American nuclear family as the model for their family life. Since then, Slovak families have typically had two or three children instead of five or more, and when children marry they no longer live at home with their parents; they may not even live nearby.

At home, Slovak Americans and Canadian Slovaks live much as their non-Slovak neighbors do, eating the same food, listening to the same music, and enjoying the same entertainment. For the most part, they prepare the traditional dishes and play the old folk tunes and dance music only on special occasions. Yet, although most Slovak families now celebrate Christmas on December 25 and include Santa Claus in their holiday lore, they still enjoy the special soups, sausages, and pastries from their homeland. Many love these dishes so much that they celebrate both on Christmas Eve (as in Slovakia) and Christmas Day. Others feast on December 6, the traditional date of Saint Nicholas's visit. The descendants of Slovak immigrants also enjoy ethnic dishes at Easter time and at wedding celebrations.

Slovaks have integrated thoroughly into mainstream American and Canadian culture, and over time their customs have become more and more like those of other Americans and Canadians. But most still carry on some of the old traditions in a modified form. They observe the same religions their ancestors did and retain an Old World respect for the aging members of their families, who live in the old neighborhoods and can still remember the "good old days," reminding today's Slovak Americans and Canadian Slovaks of their ethnicity.

Canadian Slovaks have retained more of their ethnicity than Slovak Americans because Slovak immigration to Canada took place later than immigration to the United States. In addition, the Canadian government has actively promoted a policy of multiculturalism, encouraging ethnic groups to retain their languages and customs. And because of the post–World War II influx of nationalist Slovak political refugees, the Slovak community in Canada has a stronger sense of ethnic pride. Greater numbers of Slovak Canadians speak Slovak and have established groups that preserve their native culture. For instance, the Slovak World Congress—headquartered in Toronto, Ontario—works to unite Slovak organizations throughout the Western world.

Although their situations are somewhat different, Canadian and American Slovaks are on good terms and have warm relations. They read the same Slovak news-

For his study of viral infection, Dr. Carleton Gajdusek received the Nobel Prize for Medicine from Swedish king Carl Gustaf.

papers, join the same fraternal societies, and participate in each other's cultural events. Most Canadian and American Slovaks regard the border between the two countries as artificial; some parish priests even minister on both sides of the border. Most importantly perhaps, the Slovaks have also successfully crossed another line—the line that divides ethnic groups from mainstream culture.

Four of Today's Notable Slovak Americans

While retaining their ethnic identity to a greater or lesser extent, Slovaks in North America have made some significant contributions to society at large. Dr. Carleton Gajdusek, a Slovak American, made such a tremendous contribution that he won a Nobel Prize.

Born to Slovak parents on September 9, 1923, in Yonkers, New York, he decided at the age of 10 that he wanted to become a scientist. He finished high school at 16, graduated *summa cum laude* from the University of Rochester at 19, and earned his degree from Harvard Medical School at 22.

As a biomedical scientist, Gajdusek conducted research throughout the world. In 1958 he joined the staff of the National Institutes of Health in Bethesda, Maryland. There he continued researching a disease that had attracted his attention the year before. A tribe of people on the island of New Guinea had been dying out, stricken by *kuru* (shakes or tremors). Neither Gajdusek nor his colleagues could find the cause until they looked into the tribe's practice of ritual cannibalism: Whenever members of the tribe died, their relatives ate some of their brain tissue in order to assure the immortality of the deceased's essence, or soul.

Gajdusek and his colleagues suspected that *kuru* might be transmitted through the brain tissue. To test their theory, they injected monkeys with brain cells removed from people who had died of the disease. Several

The son of Slovak immigrants, Jaroslav Pelikan is a respected and admired history professor at Yale University.

years after receiving these injections, the monkeys started dying from *kuru*. Gajdusek's group had discovered that viruses can remain dormant for a period of years before becoming active again and causing disease. As major contributors to the study of viral infection, Gajdusek and his colleague Baruch Blumberg received the 1976 Nobel Prize for Physiology and Medicine.

Slovaks in the New World have also distinguished themselves in other areas of intellectual pursuit. Foremost among them perhaps is Jaroslav J. Pelikan, Sterling Professor of History at Yale University. The son of a Lutheran pastor who had immigrated to America and the grandson of a Lutheran bishop in Slovakia, Pelikan was born on December 17, 1923, in Akron, Ohio. He taught himself to read in Slovak at the age of two and continued to exhibit a great facility for languages while attending Concordia Junior College in Fort Wayne, Indiana. By the time he graduated, in 1942, he had learned German, Latin, Greek, Croatian, Hebrew, and Syriac.

Three years later, Pelikan simultaneously received a theology degree from Concordia Seminary in Saint Louis, Missouri, earned a Ph.D. in history from the University of Chicago, and landed a teaching job at Valparaiso University in Ohio. He then went on to teach at the University of Chicago and in 1962 moved on to Yale University in New Haven, Connecticut. From 1973 through 1978, he served as dean of Yale's graduate school.

During the course of his academic career, Pelikan has written 15 books, including *The Riddle of Roman Catholicism*, which won the 1959 Abingdon Award for the best manuscript published by the Abingdon Press. In 1971 he launched an extremely ambitious five-volume research and publication project entitled *The Christian Tradition*. Three volumes of this history have already appeared. The Slovak World Congress bestowed upon him its National Award in 1973, and in 1983 the National Endowment for the Humanities selected Pelikan as its first Jefferson Lecturer.

Michael Novak's The Rise of the Unmeltable Ethnics *made a major contribution to the ethnic revival that swept North America during the 1970s.*

Another renowned Slovak-American scholar is Michael Novak, a theologian with many other interests. Born to Slovak-American parents on September 9, 1933, in Johnstown, Pennsylvania, Novak graduated *summa cum laude* from Stonehill College in Massachusetts. In 1958 he received a Bachelor of Theology degree from the Gregorian University in Rome, and in 1965 an M.A. in religious studies from Harvard University. Since then, he has taught at a number of institutions, including Harvard, and Stanford University in California. He has also written several novels and books of theology and social commentary.

A speechwriter for a number of Democratic party candidates during the early 1970s, Novak accepted a position as a syndicated columnist in 1976. In 1978 his political interests gained him a place as a resident scholar at the American Enterprise Institute for Public Policy Research in Washington, D.C. Novak supported Ronald Reagan during the 1980 presidential race, and in return he was named head of the United States delegation to the Experts' Meeting on Human Contacts of the Conference on Security and Cooperation in Europe. Truly a Slovak American of achievement, Novak received the Ellis Island Medal of Honor in 1986.

Slovaks have also met with some success in the field of entertainment. Robert Urich was born in Toronto, Ohio, on December 19, 1947, to Slovak-American parents. His father worked in the local steel mill and his mother worked in a dry-cleaning plant. Urich graduated from Florida State University and earned an M.A. in communications management from Michigan State University in 1971. While working as a sales account executive for a Chicago radio station, he started acting in productions at local theaters. In 1973, he landed a role in the Hollywood film *Bob and Carol and Ted and Alice*. Urich later appeared in the television series "S.W.A.T." (1975–76), "Tabitha" (1977–78), and "Soap" (1977–78). In 1978 he got his first starring role, in the television series "Vegas." Since 1981 he has starred in the series "Spenser for Hire."

Renewed Interest in Slovak Ethnicity

Because of their success in fields unrelated to their ethnic origins, Robert Urich, Michael Novak, Jaroslav Pelikan, and Carleton Gajdusek represent all assimilated American and Canadian Slovaks. But even as people of Slovak heritage have integrated into North American society, they have maintained links to their ancestral past. Especially since the 1970s, when American and Canadian Slovaks experienced an ethnic revival similar to that of many other ethnic groups at that time, they have renewed their interest in their heritage.

Much to the delight of their elders, young people increasingly take up the study of Slovak language, history, and literature; attend folk-dancing classes; and even visit Slovakia. The Czechoslovak government has encouraged this interest, reversing its longtime policy of hostility toward Slovaks in the West. Third- and fourth-generation Slovaks in North America have also established or reestablished groups that perform traditional Slovak dance.

Robert Urich stars in television's "Spenser for Hire."

The ethnic vitality of its Slovak citizens prompted the state of Pennsylvania to declare November 1985 Slovak Heritage Month.

In 1977 fascination with Slovak tradition led to the organization of the Slovak Studies Association. Made up of about 100 American and Canadian scholars, the association promotes and fosters interdisciplinary research, publication, and teaching of Slovak history, culture, and language throughout the world. It sponsors the participation of students of Slovak topics in scholarly conferences and helps scholars publish in the annual *Slovakia*, issued by the Slovak League of America in Middletown, Pennsylvania.

The resurgent interest in Slovak culture shown by the descendants of Slovak immigrants may establish the Slovaks as a distinct and permanent ethnic presence in North America. Slovaks themselves have historically felt divided by religious and cultural differences; in Slovakia they belonged to different classes, and as immigrants they came to the New World during various periods of history and from several culturally distinct regions of their homeland. In their adopted country, they retained many of the traditions that distinguished them from each other, and the institutions they created to preserve their culture perpetuated their differences. Having brought with them a varied cultural, religious, and linguistic heritage, the Slovaks did not feel like a unified people until they began to assimilate into a culture not their own.

Throughout their history, whenever Slovak Americans and Canadian Slovaks have set aside their differences, they have been able to work together to achieve common goals. The most notable example of this remains the role played by North American Slovaks in liberating Slovakia from Hungarian rule and in the subsequent establishment of the Czechoslovakian state. This combined effort (including their cooperation with Czech immigrants) would not have been possible in the Old World, where the barriers between Slovak subgroups were too high to be overcome. Assimilation into American and Canadian culture allowed many of the Slovaks' internal divisions to fade, making it possible for them to unite under a single banner.

Yet at the same time that assimilation has allowed Slovaks to focus on their shared heritage rather than on their differences, it threatens to obliterate Slovak ethnicity altogether. The ethnic revival will no doubt benefit the Slovak community by giving Slovaks in the United States and Canada a stronger sense of their heritage. They may finally become one Slovak people, sharing a heritage of which they are rightly proud. In a sense, Slovaks have found their true identity in North America. ✒

FURTHER READING

Balch, Emily G. *Our Slavic Fellow Citizens*. New York: Arno Press, 1969.

Bell, Thomas. *Out of This Furnace*. Pittsburgh: University of Pittsburgh Press, 1976.

Macartney, C. A. *The Hapsburg Empire, 1790–1918*. New York: Macmillan, 1969.

Novak, Michael. *The Guns of Lattimer*. New York: Basic Books, 1978.

Steiner, Eugen. *The Slovak Dilemma*. New York: Cambridge University Press, 1973.

Stolarik, M. Mark. *Growing Up on the South Side: Three Generations of Slovaks in Bethlehem, Pennsylvania, 1880–1976*. Lewisburg, PA: Bucknell University Press, 1985.

———. "Slovak Migration from Europe to North America, 1870–1918." *Slovak Studies*, Volume 20, 1980.

———. "The Slovaks." *Harvard Encyclopedia of American Ethnic Groups*. Cambridge, MA: Harvard University Press, 1980.

INDEX

Abov County, 21, 33
All Brides Are Beautiful (Bell), 89
Allies, 26
American Reformed church, 62
Amerikansko-Slovenske Noveny, 85
Austria, 17
Austrian Empire, 21, 23
Austro-Hungarian Empire, 24, 25,
    34, 63, 67

Babushka, 76
Bednarik, Charles (Chuck), 73
Bell, Thomas, 88–90
Benedictines, 64
Benes, Edvard, 28, 29
Bernolak, Anton, 22
Bohemia, 27, 28
Bosak, Michael, 38, 41, 43
Bosak State Bank, 40
Budapest, 24

Calvinism, 15, 19, 20, 47, 57, 59,
    62, 65
Canada, 36
Castle Garden, 35
Central Powers, 26
Chicago, Illinois, 36
Chicago Blackhawks, 74
child labor, 69
Christian Tradition, The (Pelikan),
    101
churches, 43, 45, 58–65, 67
Clementis, Vladimir, 30
Cleveland, Ohio, 36, 41, 47, 57
coal mines, 34, 36, 69
communism, 28–31, 84, 92
Congregation of the Vincentian
    Sisters of Charity, 64
Congregation of the Sisters of Saints
    Cyril and Methodius, 68
Counter-Reformation, 19, 20
Czech, 20, 23
Czechoslovakia, 17, 18, 23, 26, 28,
    30, 63, 75, 92, 103, 105
Czech Slavic Benevolent Society, 48

Denison Mines Limited, 42
Droppa, Cyril, 59
Dubcek, Alexander, 30, 31, 92
Duda, Andrew, 38, 39, 41, 42, 43

Ellis Island, 35
England, 27

First Catholic Slovak Ladies Union,
    57
First Catholic Slovak Union, 40, 57,
    87
First National Bank of Oliphant,
    39–40
Fitzgo, The Wild Dog of Central Park
    (Wilkes) 90
France, 26, 27
fraternal benefit societies, 14, 43,
    45–48, 57–58, 67, 72, 78, 85, 99
From This Day Forward (Bell), 89
Furdek, Stefan, 48, 57, 86, 87

Gajdusek, Carleton, 99–101, 103
Germany, 27, 29
Great Depression, 41
Great Moravia, 18
Greek Catholic church, 15, 18, 19,
    20, 47, 59, 61, 65, 84

Hitler, Adolf, 27, 28
Hlinka, Andrej, 26
hockey, 74
Hrusovsky, Frantisek, 64
Hungarian Revolution of 1848, 23
Hungary, 17, 18, 19, 21, 22, 27, 33,
    34, 39, 46, 47, 57, 62, 63, 64,
    75, 85, 86
Husak, Gustav, 30, 31
Hviezdoslav, Pavol Orszagh, 23

immigration quota system, 83
Inside Hockey (Mikita), 74
In the Midst of Life (Bell), 90
I Play to Win (Mikita), 74
Irish, 36

Jankola, Matus, 68
Jednota, 87
Jews, 20, 28, 29
Joseph II, emperor of Austria, 22

Katolik, 63
Kazinczy, Albert, 65
Kozlej, Jan, 59

Liptov County, 39, 74, 91
Luther, Martin, 19
Lutheran church, 15, 19, 20, 23, 28, 47, 57, 59, 64, 65
Lutheran Haven, Florida, 42

Magyar, 22, 23, 24, 67
Marconi, Guglielmo, 63
Masaryk, T. G., 26
Matica Slovenska, 24
Matica Slovenska v Amerike, 57
Merton by Those Who Knew Him Best (Wilkes), 91
Mexico, 91
Mikita, Stanley, 74
Moravia, 27, 28
Moscow, 29
Most, 88
Murgas, Jozef, 62, 63, 64

National Football League, 13
National Slovak Society, 48, 57, 85
Nazis, 92
News Herald, 89
Newsweek, 93
New York City, 57, 89
Nobel Prize, 99, 101
Novak, Michael, 102, 103
nuns, 64, 65, 68, 69, 70

Out of This Furnace (Bell), 89
Oviedo, 42

Pankuch, Jan, 41
parochial schools, 24, 67, 69
   Roman Catholic, 68
   Greek Catholic, 68
   Lutheran, 68

Pelikan, Jaroslav J., 101, 103
Petrovic, Alexander (Petrofi, Sandor), 23
Philadelphia Eagles, 73
Pittsburgh, Pennsylvania, 36, 85
Poland, 17, 18, 27, 28, 75
Prohibition, 41
Protestant Reformation, 19

Riddle of Roman Catholicism, The (Pelikan), 101
Roman, Stephen, 38, 39, 42, 43
Roman Catholic church, 15, 18, 20, 23, 47, 57, 59, 60, 61, 64, 65
Rovnianek, Peter V., 47, 48, 57, 85, 86, 87
Rusnak, Michael, 43
Russia, 26
Russian Empire, 34, 85

saloons, 38, 45, 65
Saris County, 21, 33, 39, 40, 59, 89
Sasek, 63
Seckar, Alvena, 91–93
serfs, 21, 23
Six American Families (Wilkes), 90
Slavia, Florida, 41
Slovak Americans
   assimilation, 14, 37, 45, 68, 70, 74, 97, 105
   christening celebrations 77, 78
   discrimination against, 74
   early immigration, 24, 33, 34, 35
   dance, 103
   diet, 71, 98
   ethnic revival, 105
   funeral customs, 78
   holiday celebrations, 78–81
   intellectuals, 13, 24, 85
   intermarriage, 75
   languages, 14, 15, 20, 22, 95, 96, 103
   music, 72
   national costume, 70
   newspapers, 14, 87, 96
   number in North America, 13
   political refugees, 13, 84

in professional sports, 72–74
traditions, 98
wedding customs, 75–77
Slovak Calvin Presbyterian Union,
57
Slovak Canadians, 43, 59, 61, 65,
69, 74, 83, 84, 98, 105
Slovak Catholic Sokol, 57
Slovak Evangelical Union, 57
Slovak Gymnastic Union Sokol, 57
Slovakia, 29, 39, 60, 64, 86
history of, 17–31
population explosion in, 20, 33
Slovakia, 104
Slovak Institute, 64
Slovak League of America, 57, 63,
104
Slovak Studies Association, 104
Slovak World Congress, 43, 98, 101
Slovenska Obrana, 40
Slovenskje Naordnje Novini, 23
Sokol, Kolomon, 91, 92
Soviet Union, 17, 28, 31
Spis County, 21, 33
Stalin, Joseph, 28, 29
steel mills, 34, 36
steerage, 35
Stur, Ludovit, 23
Sudetenland, 27

There Comes a Time (Bell), 90
Tiso, Jozef, 27, 29
Trying Out the Dream (Wilkes), 90

Ukrainians, 75
United States, 26, 33
University of Pennsylvania, 73, 92
Urich, Robert, 102, 103

Vienna, 24
Volansky, John, 61

Wilkes, Paul, 90, 91
Winnipeg, Manitoba, 83
wireless telegraphy, 63
World War I, 13, 25, 33, 35, 40, 61,
63, 73, 83, 85
World War II, 13, 15, 33, 61, 73,
74, 84, 87, 92, 96, 98

Yale University, 101
Yugoslavia, 21

Zemplin County, 21, 33
Zivena, 57
Zuska of the Burning Hills, (Seckar),
93

Picture Credits

We would like to thank the following sources for providing photographs: A. Duda & Sons, Inc., Oviedo, Florida: p. 42; Archives of Industrial Society, University of Pittsburgh: p. 64; Balch Institute for Ethnic Studies: pp. 58, 60; Marianne Barcelona: p. 93; The Bettmann Archive: pp. 16, 28, 31; Bildarchiv der Oster-reichischen Nationalbibliothek, Vienna: p. 19; Canapress Photo Service: p. 84; Culver Pictures: Cover photo and p. 77; German National Museum: p. 20; Immigration History Research Center, University of Minnesota: p. 46; Tom Kelly/PAR-NYC: pp. 49, 50 (top), 50 (bottom), 51 (top), 51 (bottom), 52 (top), 52 (bottom), 53 (top), 53 (bottom), 54 (top), 54 (bottom), 55 (top), 55 (bottom), 56, 79; Ted Kulik, Shelton, CT: pp. 94–95; Kunsthistorisches Museum, Vienna: pp. 18, 21; Library of Congress: pp. 34, 35, 38, 39; The Metropolitan Museum of Art, The Alfred Stieglitz Collection: p. 36; The Museum of Modern Art/Film Stills Archive: p. 90; New York Public Library: pp. 15, 37, 66–67, 68, 72; PAR-NYC: p. 88; Pressons Bild AB: p. 99; Public Archives of Canada: pp. 82–83; The Slovak Museum and Archives, Middletown, PA: pp. 25, 40, 47, 48, 63, 71, 80, 86, 89, 102, 104; The *Sunday Record*, Bergen/Passaic/Hudson Counties, New Jersey, photo by Bob Brush: p. 93; Katrina Thomas: p. 12; Thunder Bay Multicultural Association: pp. 44, 76; UPI/Bettmann Newsphotos: pp. 26, 27, 29, 43, 74, 75, 96; Warner Bros.: p. 103; The Western Reserve Historical Society: pp. 22, 73; John Woodruff/Public Archives of Canada: p. 32; Yale University: p. 100.

M. MARK STOLARIK, president of the Balch Institute for Ethnic Studies in Philadelphia, was born in Slovakia during World War II. He immigrated to Canada with his family and later settled in the United States, where he became a specialist in the history of immigration and ethnicity. He has published more than 20 articles and 4 books on ethnicity, including *Growing Up on the South Side: Three Generations of Slovaks in Bethlehem, Pennsylvania, 1880–1976.*

DANIEL PATRICK MOYNIHAN is the senior United States senator from New York. He is also the only person in American history to serve in the cabinets or subcabinets of four successive presidents—Kennedy, Johnson, Nixon, and Ford. Formerly a professor of government at Harvard University, he has written and edited many books, including *Beyond the Melting Pot, Ethnicity: Theory and Experience* (both with Nathan Glazer), *Loyalties,* and *Family and Nation.*